The Eleventh Commandment

The Eleventh Commandment

A Jewish Childhood in Nazi-Occupied France

Revised Edition

Leo Michel Abrami

Albion
Andalus
Boulder, Colorado
2012

"The old shall be renewed,

and the new shall be made holy."

— Rabbi Avraham Yitzhak Kook

Albion-Andalus Inc.
P. O. Box 19852
Boulder, CO 80308
www.albionandalus.com

Design and composition by Albion-Andalus, Inc.
Cover design by Sari Wisenthal-Shore.
Cover photo: Leo Abramowski.

Manufactured in the United States of America

ISBN-13: 978-0615601854
ISBN-10: 0615601855

To my brother Robert Abrami and my children,

Arianne, Dan, Linda, David, and Jonathan

— Leo Michel Abrami

vi

Contents

Acknowledgements

I WISH TO thank my wife Rosemary for her steadfast support during the writing of this book; Glen and Bobbie Zelkind for their valued friendship; and Netanel Miles-Yépez for skillfully editing the manuscript and for the production of this book.

— L.M.A.

Preface

THOUGH IT IS MORE THAN sixty years later, the memories of World War II continue to haunt me. However determined I was to erase them from my consciousness through the years, they simply would not fade away. Thus, I resolved to write this memoir in the hope that it would liberate me from the shackles of their continual recollection.

I was only a schoolboy when the German armies invaded France and imposed their terrible rule over us. At the time, some politicians thought that the people of France might be treated more favorably if they went-along and collaborated with the enemy. But the consequences were disastrous for all of us. Convinced that they were fighting a "great war" which would bring about the triumph of the Aryan race, the Nazis implemented a policy of ethnic cleansing in all the countries they conquered. Entire segments of their populations—Jews, Gypsies, Communists and members of the Underground—became targets of a systematic campaign of extermination.

Of all these groups, however, the Jews were singled-out for particularly harsh treatment. They were compelled to wear a yellow star on the left side of their garments and were subject to mercilessly restrictive rules, designed to engender the scorn and contempt of their fellow citizens. Many were arrested by the police and deported to concentration camps in Poland and Germany where most were ruthlessly murdered. The persecution went on until the very end of the war, by which time, over eighty thousand Jews had been deported from France.

One of the only ways to avoid this fate was to go into hiding in the French countryside. That is what my mother did for my younger brother and me; she arranged for us to live with farmers in Normandy — my brother on one farm and I on another — where we remained until the liberation of France by the Allies. The farmers were not told that we were Jewish, and we were instructed never to reveal this fact to anyone, under any circumstances, so as not to endanger either them or us. Thus we hid our Jewish identity in our hearts and pretended to be good Christians, like all the other children of the area.

Eventually, these experiences motivated me to look deeply into my Jewish roots and later to train as both a cantor and a rabbi. But now, looking back on a long career as a rabbi in the United States, I wish to revisit the terrain of my childhood and the decisions that were made for me then. I wish to express my gratitude to all the people of good will who protected and nurtured me through the most difficult period in my life. Most of all, I wish to pay homage to my mother for her amazing courage in the face of adversity, and her devotion to her parents and her children; for she is, without doubt, the real hero of this story.

— Leo Michel Abrami
Sun City West, Arizona, January 1ˢᵗ, 2012

Leo Abramowski in 1941 or 1942.

1

Bagnolet

VAS-T-EN, SALE JUIF et retourne dans ton pays! — yelled one of my classmates. "Go back to your own country, dirty Jew!"

"My *own* country?" I asked myself, confused.

At the time, I was only eight years old, a third grader at the Ecole Sadi-Carnot in Bagnolet, a suburb near the center of Paris. I knew well enough that I was being insulted, but for the life of me, I could not comprehend — *What for?*

As I walked home that day, I wondered what he had meant by "your own country." Had I not been born in France like him? And as for being "dirty," I knew this was simply untrue; after all, I showered at the public baths once a week like everyone else in our neighborhood! So what was he talking about?

As for being a "Jew," I still had no clear idea of what that meant. My mother had tried to explain it to my brother and me, but I couldn't understand how our being "the descendants of the Israelites of biblical times" had anything to do with all of these threats and insults.

World War II had just broken out and the German invasion of Central and Western Europe was underway. The Nazi leaders accused the Jews of having fomented the war for their own benefit and the newspapers were full of grotesque caricatures of Jews — with crooked noses and heavy lips — conspiring to establish dominion over France and the entire world. On the radio, the announcers kept repeating: "Jews live like parasites in the midst of our society; they have betrayed our trust and cannot be allowed to rule over us."

Hearing these diatribes, I somehow felt ashamed of belonging to a people that was regarded with such contempt by so many people, but I also wondered how any of it could possibly be true; after all, no one I knew, and certainly no one in my own family had ever been guilty of anything that would justify their calling us "traitors."

With the exception of my grandparents, we had all been born in France and knew no other allegiance. And though my grandparents were natives of Latvia who had settled in Paris at the turn of the century, they had made France their home, just as our Spanish neighbors had done when they fled Spain during its civil war. Indeed, on my street alone, there were immigrants from many different countries—Russia, Poland, Spain, Italy and Belgium. So why were we being singled out?

I reasoned that because our family name was Abramowski, this probably sounded both Russian and Jewish at the same time, opening us up to twice the suspicion of "foreignness" and divided loyalties.

But how could my grandfather, my beloved *zeide*, have been a traitor? There seemed to be no greater patriot in our neighborhood than Leib Abramowski who had volunteered to serve in the French army during World War I and who been decorated for his courage. At his funeral, I saw how the other veterans of the "Great War" paid homage to him and expressed the gratitude of the French people for his willingness to join the army of his own free will, even though he had been born in Latvia. All of these soldiers recognized that he and his family had 'chosen' to become citizens of France and to fight for its liberty; so why couldn't our neighbors see this?

2

My *zeide* was the son of a rabbi, but had decided to forgo the rabbinate in order to pursue a trade instead, learning to install central heating systems in people's homes. After moving to France as a young man, he volunteered for service in World War I and was assigned to a unit in charge of the maintenance and repair of military equipment, where he spent three years repairing cannons and small arms near the front.

Carlotta "Lotta" Abramowski, my grandmother, whom I called *bubbeh*, was just as industrious as my grandfather. Though she hadn't been able to attend school in her village, at eighteen, she hired a private tutor and learned to read and write Hebrew, Yiddish and Russian in her spare time. When I knew her, she always kept a book near-to-hand so she could read a few pages whenever she had a free moment. On the Jewish New Year and other holidays, she always invited a few neighbors to our home and read them some of the prayers and their interpretations in Yiddish.

My mother, Anna, had been born in Paris in 1903. She went to public school, and though she did not go to the university, she attended night classes and lectures at various institutions for many years. She was a person of profound intelligence, compassion and character. She took care of each of her parents until their dying day and raised my brother and me at the same time, all while working to support the entire family.

She had met my father while on vacation in Nice, on the French Riviera, where he had been invited to give a cello recital at the main synagogue on the occasion of its formal rededication. They were married a few weeks later and I was born in Paris the following year. Sadly, their marriage didn't last and they were separated while my mother was still pregnant with my younger brother.

Sometimes I asked my mother about him, but there was not much she could tell me and I did not wish to cause her any pain by pressing the subject.

At school, when my classmates would ask about my father, I would tell them that he had died shortly after I was born; I didn't know how to explain that my parents had "separated" and that I had not heard from my father since.

At the onset of the war, my mother, my younger brother and I were living with my maternal grandparents in a two-story brick house that *zeide* had built himself in this eastern suburb of Paris. Like all the children in my neighborhood, I went to public school during the day and played in the street outside my home in the afternoon.

After school, *bubbeh* watched over my brother and me while my mother worked in the city. On Monday afternoons, however, my mother would come home early to take me to the *Fleishmann Beth Ha-Midrash*, a small Jewish academy and synagogue in the Marais, what was then the Jewish quarter of Paris, for a private lesson.

My tutor was an elderly Russian Jew with a white beard and a black *yarmulke* who would teach me the letters of the Hebrew alphabet. Occasionally, he fell asleep in the middle of a lesson and, upon awaking, asked me to remind him of where we were in our book before he had dozed off. In a few months I had memorized the entire Hebrew alphabet and was just ready to begin the study of the Torah when news of the coming war forced us to postpone my lessons.

My mother was then working as a sales clerk in a fashionable clothing store owned by a cousin of ours. On Thursdays, when I had no school, I would sometimes accompany her to the store where I would read and play in the small office in the back. At the end of the day, she would close-up and we would go to the market to buy a little food before returning home.

On weekends, the whole family would often go to a park for a few hours, where my *bubbeh* would sit on a bench and knit socks for her grandchildren and my mother would watch us while we played on the swings or merry-go-round.

This was the simple and happy routine of our lives before the war began.

11

The German Invasion

AS SOON AS I was old enough to read the headlines, I noticed a single name appearing more and more frequently on the front page of the newspapers—*Adolf Hitler*. Often below this headline were a few paragraphs in heavy black print accompanied by a photo of an angry looking man and a map of Europe with big black arrows pointing East and West.

Ignoring earlier promises, Hitler had declared war on Poland and invaded the country with an unexpected *Blitzkrieg*—a 'lightning war' that caught the Poles utterly by surprise. The Germans then turned to the West and invaded Holland and Belgium, moving inexorably toward France with virtually no resistance.

At the time, I was too young to grasp the gravity of these events, but was aware that nerves were strained in the people all around me, and that they talked of these events with worried faces and fear in their voices.

Eventually, the German troops crossed the Maginot Line—a sophisticated underground fortification built to protect France against an invasion from the East—and advanced into French territory. The French army was unable to forestall the invasion and many soldiers were captured or simply fled the battlefields in terror. The newspapers and the radio were foretelling the imminent defeat of France and warning people to prepare for difficult times.

As the German troops approached Paris in May of

1940, I could hear the thundering sounds of war just outside the capital and watched as a panic set in among the city's inhabitants. Many people simply packed-up and fled, while others sent their children away to the relative 'safety' of the countryside.

My mother was also afraid and arranged for my brother and me to go to a summer camp on an island off the southwest coast of France.

Early one morning, she took us to the train station, where we joined hundreds of other children all bound for the island of Oléron on the way to Bordeaux. I had never traveled by train before and the whole journey seemed like a great adventure. During the trip, which lasted almost an entire day, I saw more of the French countryside than I had ever seen before. We passed by towns and villages with houses clustered around tall and beautiful churches, and meadows where the cattle grazed peacefully, seemingly ignorant of the war that had engulfed the rest of France.

We arrived in La Rochelle in the late afternoon and continued our journey in buses. A ferry then took us to the island of Oléron, just a few miles from the mainland.

The island was surrounded by the immaculate blue waters of the Atlantic and edged by beaches of golden sand. Beyond the beaches were green fields and small woods, and a few villages with scattered houses here and there. I had never seen such a wonder of nature and peace before. It looked like pictures I had seen in magazines at school but which I could hardly conceive of as really existing somewhere.

The camp was not meant to accommodate so many children, but under the circumstances, the organizers did their best to house all of the little-refugees who had arrived from the capital. Right away, we were each assigned a cot in the middle of a large dormitory and told to prepare for the night. We put our clothes and other personal possessions under our cots, as there was hardly any space to walk between them. Then we waited in line to go to the bathroom and to wash our hands before going to the dining hall. There were two separate dinners that night; the dining hall was also too small to hold all of us at the same time.

The next day, and almost every day after, we walked three-by-three to the beach, merrily singing folk songs as we went. Once there, we played for hours, building sandcastles and looking for seashells. Under the supervision of our counselors, some of us ventured into the water, but most of the children my age didn't go very far because none of us, being children from the city, had learned to swim yet. Everybody knew that the war continued just off the coast, but here on the sunny beach, everything seemed perfect.

This bliss continued for about a week before I was once again reminded of the war outside and how it was somehow bound up with my being Jewish. One day, we were assembled in the main hall when the director of our sports activities called my name and asked me to come forward. With some trepidation, I went to stand next to him in front of all the assembled children. Then, to my horror, he began to speak disparagingly of the Jews and suddenly pulled my shorts down, exposing me in front of everyone! He said, "You see, he is a *Jew* whose foreskin has been removed." The children burst out laughing as I stood there naked in front of them, shocked and trembling.

The sports director, it turned out, was a member of one of the early French militia groups that endorsed the Nazi ideology and willingly collaborated with them. The most prominent of these at the time was the Service d'Ordre Legionnaire, which was later absorbed into the

Milice Française, a paramilitary force formed by the Vichy government to fight the French Resistance. It must have been my surname that made him suspect that I was Jewish. Pulling my pants down was just his way of proving it and humiliating me in front of the other children; for in those days, only Jews were circumcised.[*]

Surprisingly, not a single counselor or member of the staff came forward to comfort me or to ask me if I was alright. No one said a word about it. Now I know they were afraid of challenging the sports director for fear of being denounced as 'Jewish sympathizers' to the authorities. I was left to deal with the pain and humiliation on my own, and in my lonely isolation, with burning tears, I asked God to protect me from wicked people who wished to harm me for no reason.

After this demonstration of hatred, the instructor left me alone and the children seemed to forget that it had ever happened. We stayed on at the camp for another two months before being returned to our respective families in Paris. By then, the German military forces had tightened their grip on the northern part of the country and all military resistance came to a halt. We all realized now that we would have to learn to live under a German occupation.

After we returned to the city, the French authorities, acting on behalf of the Germans, ordered all Jews to register at City Hall. I accompanied my mother to the Office of the Civil Registry in Bagnolet, where the clerk asked my mother to fill-out a questionnaire and present her identity card. He stamped it with the word *Juif*, 'Jew,' and told us we could leave.

---

[*] After the war, I learned that this instructor volunteered to serve in the German army and was never heard from again.

10

A few weeks later, the authorities issued a number of ordinances meant to restrict the movements of the Jews in Paris. We were not allowed to walk in the streets of certain neighborhoods, to enter movie theaters, concert halls, museums and sports arenas, or travel outside the city without a permit. We could enter shops only at specific hours: food markets between eleven and twelve in the morning, and other stores between three and four in the afternoon (when much of what one could buy with or without ration coupons had long since been sold).

Mother and I would often get up before dawn to go to the open market in defiance of the new ordinances, sometimes waiting in line for hours in front of a stall to buy a fish or a few vegetables. Most everything else was rationed now and we needed coupons to buy such staples as bread and cheese.

One morning, my mother awoke early and noticed that my brother, Robert, was nowhere to be found. She looked in his room, in the courtyard and in the street, but there was no trace of him. Then it occurred to her that he might have gone by himself to the Thursday open market. So she rushed to the market, located near City Hall, and found him waiting in line, half asleep and barely standing on his feet. He had wanted to surprise us all with fish for our *Shabbat* dinner. Much relieved, my mother got into line with him, warmed him up, and stayed with him until he was able to buy the fish with the pocket money he had saved for this purpose.

Worse than the ordinances that affected our ability to shop were those that affected our livelihood; for another ordinance prohibited Jews from owning a business or holding gainful employment. It was actually illegal for Jews to work! Jewish-owned shops and factories were seized and the authorities appointed new, so-called 'Aryan' owners and administrators in their stead. As a result, our cousin Maurice, who owned the clothing shop in which my mother worked, was compelled to turn over his property to the government and my mother lost her job. Before long, our meager savings were used up and we really began to struggle. As the sole support of our family, my mother would have to find some other way to keep us alive.

She was not alone in this situation though; virtually every Jewish family we knew suffered similarly from these anti-Semitic ordinances. Then as now, I could hardly conceive of how a liberal country like France could so easily agree to impose such unjust policies upon its citizens. But the Germans had succeeded in this, *not* because of any outright coercion, but largely because they did not have to convince the members of the puppet government. Xenophobia and hatred of Jews had been endemic in France for generations; thus, one only needed to fan the flames of these old hatreds— promulgating the outright lies of the fictitious *Protocols of the Elders of Zion*, a document detailing a Jewish conspiracy to achieve world domination, long since proven to be an anti-Semitic hoax—to achieve their ends.

In order to maintain some sense of normalcy, and to keep up our courage, we often poked fun at these ridiculous accusations in the privacy of our homes. Humorous anecdotes and jokes also began to circulate among us, usually making light of the desperate situation of those Jews who were looking for work when it was illegal to do so! One of these jokes, probably the first I ever heard, is still with me to this day:

Anxious to find a job, a Jew sees a sign in front of a circus tent advertising dangerous work—"Seeking courageous men for part-time work. Cowards need not apply."

Though not necessarily courageous, he has no other choice; he puts his shoulders back and enters the tent. There he meets the circus master who asks him, "Sir, are you an intrepid man, unafraid of danger?"

The Jew answers: "Sir, I am ready to do anything to earn a living. So I'll be as courageous as I need to be!"

"Fine," says the circus master, "In that case, I'll tell you why I need a courageous man. As you may have seen from the billboard outside, I've announced a fight between two lions for tonight's program. The problem is, one of my lions is sick, and so I'll need you to fill-in for the lion. I'll give you a lion-suit to wear and teach you how to walk and talk like a real lion. And when you're attacked, I'll also need you to fight like a lion. Of course, I realize that this is dangerous, but the pay is good — five hundred francs a night! Are you still willing to take the job?"

The Jew thinks for a moment and then accepts the offer. What else can he do? He and his family will starve otherwise. So he is coached for an hour or so on how to act like a lion and told to get ready for the show.

When the show starts, he is dressed and quivering in his lion-suit. He listens as the band plays a fanfare and the circus master announces the main event — "A battle between two lions!" He thinks he's going to be sick. The first lion enters the arena and walks slowly to the center of the circle. Then the handlers open his cage and he starts to walk cautiously toward the other lion. As he nears the lion, he is so terrified that he begins to recite the Shema, as a Jew should before he dies. But even as he is saying, "Hear, O Israel," he hears a muffled sound *coming from the other lion, "the Lord is our God, the Lord is One!"*

We all laughed at this, attempting to find some comfort in these jokes about our own desperation.

Throughout this period, the Nazis and their French collaborators continued to add insult to injury, spreading the most absurd lies about us. They accused us of showing "contempt and ingratitude" to this wonderful country that had welcomed us with such hospitality. My mother was quick to dismiss this hateful propaganda, telling my brother and I that Jews were loyal citizens of France and would never show contempt for those who had received them so kindly when they had arrived as penniless immigrants. She then told us about the many valuable contributions Jews had made to France in science and medicine, manufacturing and commerce.

As children constantly exposed to a barrage of this propaganda, we were amazed to hear how a Jewish baron, James (Jakob) Mayer Rothschild had established hospitals and clinics, homes for the aged, orphanages and welfare organizations all over France; and how the Eiffel Tower—which we had only seen in pictures as we were not allowed to go near it—had been designed and built by Alexandre-Gustave Eiffel, who was believed by some to be Jewish. In this way, my mother did her best to counter the effect this propaganda was having on us, telling us to ignore these vicious lies as just that.

"The war will soon come to an end," she would say, "and we will be able to resume a normal life. Let us pray for all those who are suffering at his time, those who are languishing in forced labor camps, and for those who are courageously fighting to bring an end to the war."

No matter what our circumstances, my mother always seemed to have the attitude that it shouldn't interfere with what her children needed. So, in spite of the hardships we were suffering at the time, she somehow managed to arrange piano lessons for me with Mademoiselle Baudoire, the music teacher who lived across the street. Of course, this couldn't last, and only two months later, we were forced to sell our piano and I to abandon the music lessons I loved so much. Our main task consisted in finding ways to survive. But whenever I thought about it later, I said to myself—"It's Hitler's fault that I cannot play the piano better than I do!"

Since she could not work legally, my mother sold all of our valuables in order to put food on the table. The jewelry was first to go, then the antiques and furniture which my grandparents had accumulated over a lifetime. When these were gone, my mother had to get more creative. She started collecting discarded newspapers, rags and pieces of metal and glassware from garbage cans on the street. Often, I accompanied her on these early morning foraging missions through the neighborhood, after which, we would bring everything that we had collected back to our courtyard, where we piled them in a little shack. Then, once a week, we carted them off to a recycling center to sell, usually earning enough money to live modestly for another week.

Even with money, though, you couldn't just buy food at will. The prices on the black market were very high and we couldn't afford to squander the little money we had earned on anything that wasn't an absolute necessity. On the other hand, the food we were allowed to buy with our ration stamps wasn't sufficient to keep us from hunger. So my mother decided to go to Les

Halles, the main distribution center of fruits and vegetables for Paris, once or twice a week in order to find additional food for us.

Often, it happened that a shipment of fruits or vegetables would arrive in Paris partly spoiled. So the truck drivers would simply dump their cargo on the ground, leaving beggars and other hungry Parisians like us to search through the heaps of rotten fruit in search of something that might still be safe to eat. This was not a pleasant task, and few were willing to resort to this way of collecting food, considering it too humiliating; but my mother would not hesitate to join the beggars if it meant that we might get what we needed in order to live through the food shortages.

During this period, we defied the restrictive ordinances whenever we thought we could get away with it. It was simply a necessity of survival. So even though Jews could not be lawfully employed, my mother managed to find work as a part-time sales clerk in a dress-shop. Apparently, German soldiers were more and more frequently coming into the store to buy dresses for their wives and daughters back home, so the owner felt he needed to hire someone who could speak German, which my mother could. Of course, he knew that it was illegal to hire a Jewish employee, but the need to earn a living seemed to outweigh the risk for him. My mother only hoped that none of our neighbors would denounce her to the police. In the meantime, she easily passed for a Gentile to the store's German patrons.

Once, a uniformed German soldier looking at dresses casually told my mother that he had been an electrician before being drafted into the army. My mother then told him that we had an electrical problem at home and were having difficulties finding a repairman to fix it. Without the slightest hesitation, the

16

German soldier offered to help and agreed to come to our home to fix the problem. He waited for her to finish her shift and then the two of them walked back to our house.

When I saw the soldier in his green uniform entering our apartment, I thought that he had come to arrest us! But my mother seemed calm and was speaking to him in a friendly manner, so I relaxed and watched what was going on. The soldier went straight to the meter and repaired the electrical circuit in just a few seconds. We thanked him, and my mother walked him back to the main thoroughfare where they took leave of one other.

Our neighbors could not believe their eyes! They knew my mother was not the kind of woman to have a fleeting affair with a German soldier, or to become a "horizontal collaborator," as the phrase went in those days. But what else could account for what they had seen? There remained only one other possibility—she must have acted as an informer for the German authorities. Oddly enough, this mistaken assumption likely deterred them from denouncing her to the police through the weeks and months that followed.

My mother was constantly teaching us through her own example that one should be daring and never give the impression of being afraid of people or circumstances. She would say: "It's like coming face to face with a ferocious dog. If you run away because you're frightened, the dog is likely to run after you and attack you; but if you just walk calmly by, with assurance and resolution, he'll probably let you go on in peace."

III
Arrests and Deportations

IN MAY OF 1941, at the request of the German authorities, the French police began arresting Jewish men on a selective basis. The first apprehended were foreigners—Poles, Czechs and former Austrians—who were now declared stateless, as well as any foreign man who did not possess a French passport.

At first, they only arrested men—whether married or not—who were between eighteen and forty; but later, they also began to take men up to sixty years old. The officials claimed that these men were needed as workers in German factories, apparently to replace those who had been drafted into the army. Of course this was a lie, or at least, only partially true.

These men were either arrested in their homes or summoned to the police station for a supposed verification of their identities. In most cases, they were detained there and never allowed home, even to collect their belongings. From the police station, they were sent to various gathering-points, and eventually to one or another of the concentration camps French authorities had established some fifty miles south of Paris.

A few months later, Theodor Dannecker, the officer in charge of Jewish affairs for the Gestapo, declared that all Jews were Communists and agents of Stalin. And before long, the Germans ordered the arrest of all Jewish women who were not French citizens as well. But the French police showed even greater eagerness to comply with this order and forcefully arrested entire families, including pregnant women and babies, taking them all to the camps.

In their official notices, the authorities claimed that these families were being "relocated" in Germany; but after the liberation of France, we learned that the expression *"relocated in the East"* was simply a code used by the Germans to mean *'exterminated'* in the death camps.

Of course, it was not long before naturalized citizens of Jewish descent and their families were also arrested. The police simply selected their names and addresses from the lists that had been made the year before, after the Jews were ordered to register at City Hall.

Soon, we were tracked through the city like game in the forest. Any person caught transgressing one of the regulations applying to the Jews, whether intentionally or by mistake, was automatically arrested and deported to a concentration camp. The authorities accepted no excuses or extenuating circumstances. Thus, we hoped and prayed that no one would denounce us to the police for such an infraction; for any accusation, whether true or false, might have the most tragic consequences.

Fortunately we were blessed with a kind and compassionate neighbor—Madame Paquet. Though she was Jewish by birth, her husband was Catholic and she had deliberately refused to declare herself a Jew after the German occupation began. No one knew that she was Jewish except my mother, and she would make sure not to be seen speaking to my mother in public, so as to avoid any suspicion falling on her. Nevertheless, she continued to invite my mother into her home after nightfall so that they might be able to have friendly conversations in private.

After these visits, my mother would return home reassured about our immediate future. For Madame Paquet was often well-informed about the intentions of the Paris police because her husband's close connections with several policemen. And whenever new arrests of Jews were being planned in our neighborhood, she always warned us well ahead of time. In turn, my mother would inform our Jewish friends who would then go into hiding immediately.

Before the French government had decided to arrest French-born Jews, we had felt relatively safe; though we knew it was only a matter of time before the police began to arrest all the Jews in order to meet the quotas set up by the Nazis. When this situation became a reality, we came to rely on the information Madame Paquet gave us to avoid arrest and deportation. Because of this, we began to think seriously of how we might escape. Even my grandmother, who had no desire to move from her house, had agreed that she might come with us if the situation got any worse.

French citizens were encouraged to report any Jews or members of the Underground who were hiding in various parts of the city. And unfortunately, there were citizens who thought it was their duty to obey this law, and who did not hesitate to call the police and inform on their neighbors. In this way, many innocent people were tracked down and deported to concentration camps. The authorities rewarded the informers for their cooperation with a 100 francs for an individual, and mere 200 hundred for an entire family!

One morning, we were awakened very early by a commotion in the street outside of our apartment. A number of uniformed policemen and inspectors in civilian clothes had just arrived in a patrol car. One of them held a list in his hands of those who were to be arrested on our street.

They would enter a building, knock loudly on the door of an apartment and shout—"Open up, Police!" and give the family two minutes to gather a few belongings and put them in a bag or a suitcase. These unfortunates were then told to walk toward the city buses, which had been requisitioned by the police for the purpose of transporting them to designated gathering-points. I watched in horror as the children cried and the elderly—who had difficulty walking—were ordered to walk faster. *"Vite, plus vite!"* the policemen shouted.

We watched all this in consternation from behind the curtains of our second floor apartment. Expecting to be the next, my mother quickly packed a small suitcase for my brother and me, my grandmother and herself. I can still remember the voice of the concierge of the building facing ours—a middle-aged woman wearing a grey peasant dress—asking the policeman in charge, "Aren't you going to arrest these *kikes?*" pointing to the windows of our apartment. She told him our name and the officer checked his list. "No Madame; not this time."

My friend, Jacques, and his entire family, were arrested that day. More than anything, I wanted to say goodbye to him, but my mother stopped me, saying: "They must not know that we are here." Jacques and I had walked to school together every day. After the arrest, I never saw him or any of his family again.

Our neighbors, who also witnessed these arrests, reacted in different ways to these scenes of horror: some were visibly upset and saddened; a few seemed to be pleased at the sight; but the majority didn't show any particular emotion. In wartime, people become accustomed to the unusual, to the point that even the arrest of innocent children and the elderly does not shock them anymore.

Because of the sustained propaganda on the radio

and in the press, many had come to believe the false accusations spread about the Jews. Or maybe it was simply what they were already disposed to believe. Others, however, who had closer relationships with Jews knew that this propaganda was a lie. But the majority did not seem to care one way or another.

As I said before, I didn't really understand what it was to be Jewish yet, nor how this fact coincided with my grandparents having been Russian immigrants, and still less why this particular heritage singled us out for such extreme prejudice. After all, France had been a 'melting pot' of cultures and nationalities for centuries, and even Napoleon's parents were not French, but Italian. If the French government had not purchased the island of Corsica two years before he was born, the future emperor might never have ruled over France and a large portion of Europe.

I had also learned in my history class that the original people of France, or Gaul, as it was then known, were Celts who had been vanquished by the Roman *consul* Julius Caesar sometime before the beginning of the Christian era. And, of course, the Romans brought with them their own language, which became the basis for much of modern French. Later, the territory was successively invaded by Visigoths, Alemanni, Vandals, Huns, Burgundians and Franks, all of which intermarried with the native Gauls and added something to the culture.

Thus, our teacher made it clear that there was no racially pure strain in the French population; for France had emerged from a cross-breeding of many different ethnic and racial groups. So why should it matter then if three-hundred-and-fifty-thousand descendants of the people of the Bible had also adopted France as their home?

I was confused about the meaning of the Republican motto—*Liberté, égalité, fraternité*—inscribed on the facade of every public building in the country; for we were being denied all of these rights. We were treated as pariahs and criminals, arrested and deported, simply for being descended from one of the oldest peoples in the world. Until this point, I had believed that the duty of the police was to maintain law and order in the country, to protect the innocent and to prevent criminals from perpetrating acts of violence. Why then were they arresting children who could not possibly have committed a crime? These things were never discussed in our classes at school and I was left to figure them out for myself.

Even though I had never been afraid of death, not in any real sense, I was frightened by the thought of being sent to a land of perdition where I and my family might disappear from the face of the earth. After all, friends and neighbors were taken away continually and were never heard from again.

But what was most disturbing was the way in which the police were intervening in our lives and taking us from our neighborhoods; for they did so systematically, according to a carefully planed procedure that was elaborated by the authorities under the supervision of a representative of the Nazi Commander in charge of Jewish Affairs. Even more regrettable was the fact that they were using information *we* had provided them a year earlier when we were asked to register at City Hall. Their leaders must have known at the time that they would use this information to arrest the Jews of France and send them to concentration camps.

At the time, we were unaware of the "final solution," that the ultimate goal of the Nazis was the extermination of all European Jews. Of course, there were rumors to that effect circulating Paris, but we could not force ourselves to believe that such a cold and brutal scheme was possible, even for the Nazis.

On the 16th and 17th of July, 1942, the police arrested over eight thousand Jews in Paris alone. They took them to various police stations and parking lots, and from there to a dilapidated sports arena, the *Vélodrome d'hiver*, which had been built for twelve thousand spectators. The detainees could not believe what was happening to them. They had been taken from their homes early that morning and were now locked up in the most squalid conditions. They had not committed any crime, but were nevertheless treated as criminals.

At the *Vel d'Hiv*, as it was called, the facilities were woefully inadequate for such a mass of people. Its few toilets were soon clogged as there was practically no water in the building. There was no medical assistance for the detainees; for, even if some of them happened to be doctors and nurses, they were unable to help those in need of urgent care because they had no supplies of any kind. Nor was there any food or water for several days, not until a few religious groups and charitable organizations like the Quakers and the Catholic Welfare Association received permission to bring in small quantities of food.

As a result of this cruel and inhumane treatment, dozens of people died in these squalid conditions, while others simply committed suicide. At the same time, a number of children were born in this terrible environment, in the worst possible conditions, not knowing what awaited them in the weeks and months to come.

The police were ill prepared to handle a mass arrest of this kind and had no idea what to do with so many prisoners. It took them five days before they finally decided to expand the concentration camp on the outskirts of Paris, in the suburb of Drancy. This is what came to be called the *Raffle du Vel d'Hiv*.

The camp was situated some six or seven miles north of Paris—almost halfway between the city and the present location of the Charles De Gaulle Airport—in a complex of apartment buildings which had been declared unsafe and left unfinished. Windows and doors had not yet been installed and there were only a few partially completed bathrooms on every floor. Most of the Jews arrested in Paris and its immediate environs were taken to this camp.

My uncle, Michel, and his son Gabriel, who was only seventeen years old, were arrested and taken to the Drancy camp. My aunt Fanny tried everything she could think of to free them. She even agreed to work for the UGIF, the Union Générale des Israélites de France, under the control of the Commissariat on Jewish Affairs, because she had been told that by so doing, she might be able to obtain the release of her son. And, after much effort, including bribes to several French and German officials, she eventually succeeded in obtaining his freedom. The moment my cousin Gabriel was freed from the Drancy camp, he joined the Maquis (French resistance), and on several occasions was decorated by the officers of the FFI (French Free Forces).

It was not uncommon for the Germans to use deceit to accomplish their mission. They continually made promises to Jews who agreed to collaborate with them, telling them that they would not be deported. But they only used them for information and delayed their deportation for six months or a year and sent them to the camps like all the rest.

They took the same approach in the concentration camps and in all the factories where they used slave laborers. Oskar Schindler was one of the few German industrialists who protected his Jewish workers from deportation. When some of them were arrested and sent to Auschwitz, he pleaded with the German authorities and managed to have them returned to his factories.

When my aunt Fanny became aware of the danger of this unspoken, collaborationist policy, she resigned from her post at the UGIF in Paris and went into hiding in the countryside. She worked in a restaurant for two years and was thus able to survive the war. Her husband who had been deported to the East was killed in the camps.

IV
Under the Occupation

THE FOOD RATIONING at this time was so severe that we were continually looking for ways to supplement our meager diet. Thus, my mother and I would go to the open market in the next town — arriving early in the morning and waiting in line for an hour or two — hoping to purchase some fruits or vegetables when the merchants arrived with their produce.

Fortunately, the market was some distance from our home and no one ever recognized us. But even if they had, they probably wouldn't have said anything. After all, most of us were in the same situation, trying to stave off hunger while not attracting the attention of the authorities. Social barriers tend to vanish when you're standing in the same line.

The moment we returned home from the market, I would grab my bag with my notebooks and go off to school. Despite rising so early, to the best of my recollection, I never fell asleep during a class. This was probably because I liked Monsieur Marin, my fifth grade teacher.

Monsieur Marin was a veteran of World War I and had nothing but contempt for the German occupation forces and the French puppet-government they had installed. Of course, he was extremely careful not to state his opinions explicitly, for one of the students might report his comments to his parents who might in turn denounce him to the police.

My mother knew his wife, Mrs. Marin, because they had gone to school together. So whenever they met, they would greet each other with a big smile and exchange a few words, which would always make my mother happy.

As we were approaching the end of the school year, Monsieur Marin devoted an entire session to the question of vocational training, because the French educational system required students to make an initial decision at that stage. "You must make the right choice" he said, "so that you may engage in the proper educational track as early as possible."

I didn't know what I wanted to be as an adult, but I thought I might prefer a liberal profession to being a plumber like my grandfather. Monsieur Marin suggested I pursue secondary studies at College Turgot (now a *lycée*) in Paris, because there was no high school in our suburb. He was kind enough to give me a letter of recommendation and said I should meet with the registrar of the college in the next few days.

Since my mother was working and did not have the time to take me, I went into Paris by myself. I walked to the nearby underground station at the Porte des Lilas, one of the gates of Paris, and bought a ticket for the *metro*. When I got on, I made sure to sit in the last car — as required by the special regulations — and waited until we reached the station — Place de la République.

From there, I walked another five or six minutes until I came to an impressive grey stone building which bore the name "College Turgot" on its facade. It was situated in the heart of a busy area in Paris near a square where the Statue of Liberty was originally constructed.

The registrar was very kind. He didn't ask why I had come unaccompanied or make any comment about my name sounding Polish and Jewish, as others often did. I simply handed him the certificate my teacher had given me and was asked to fill out the questionnaire for new students. And just like that, I was registered for the coming term.

At the ceremony that concluded the school year, I received a prize for academic achievement. It was a biography of the French composer, Jacques Offenbach, whose operettas had been so popular. When the official ceremony was over, Monsieur Marin took me aside and whispered while pointing to the book, "Abramowski, you will be glad to know that the composer Offenbach was also a Jew."

I responded, "Thank you, *professeur;* it was thoughtful of you to tell me."

And that was the truth. At that time, it was reassuring to know that there were actually people who did not think badly of Jews and who recognized the valuable contributions they had made to Western culture.

I spent a good part of that summer in the small orchard my grandfather had bought before I was born. The orchard was situated about a mile from our home and contained thirty pear trees, two apple trees and a cherry tree. When the fruits were ripe, we picked them ourselves and mother took them to barter for bread or cheese or other strictly rationed items we needed.

The orchard was surrounded by a wood fence, which separated it from the houses in the next lot and kept out any unwanted thieves who might be passing by. Nevertheless, when the fruits were beginning to ripen, some of our neighbors climbed the fence at night and stole whatever fruits were within in their reach.

To protect our crop, I often spent the night in the orchard, sleeping on a bench with my dog, Fleurette, from which we kept an eye on our property. Whenever would-be-marauders climbed the fence in the dark, Fleurette would hear them and begin to bark as I mustered the courage to shout, "Who's there!?" Fleurette usually took care of any chasing that was necessary.

One night, Fleurette started barking and I immediately woke up. I grabbed my flashlight and a stick and ran after him. A teenage neighbor had put a ladder to the fence and was picking our fruit when Fleurette began to bark loudly. Startled, he dropped his bag on our side of the fence and jumped from the ladder, falling to the ground on the other side.

Hearing the noise, his father came out of the house in his pajamas and put him back on his feet. I picked up the bag of pears and threw it to his father who muttered a few words of apology. I certainly didn't want anyone stealing our fruit, but I also understood. In ordinary times, the boy probably wouldn't done it (except out of simple boyhood mischief); but in those days, we were all suffering from the shortages brought on by the war and sometimes did things we wouldn't have done otherwise. As far as I know, he never tried to steal our fruit again.

My mother and I had also planted a little vegetable garden in front of the trees. We fertilized the ground with manure and watered the plants regularly and thus we had our own 'Victory garden' that produced a portion of the fresh vegetables we needed. We harvested these vegetables the whole summer.

We were paying a special attention to our tomato plants which were doing well. Eventually they began to turn red and we decided that they would probably be ripe in two or three days. But when I returned to the orchard the next day, I found that someone else had been monitoring their progress, for all the tomatoes were gone! I was furious, but my mother was not.

"Leo," she said, "you must understand that many people go to bed hungry these days, and it is difficult for them to resist the temptation to steal food when it is so close to hand, even in the garden next door. Don't worry about it; we will barter pears for tomatoes."

Sometimes my mother was altruistic to the point of forgetting her own needs. She believed that Providence would guide her to the proper path and would eventually show us a way of getting what we needed.

In the autumn, I began attending College Turgot in Paris and became accustomed to the new system of having a different teacher for every subject. During the breaks, the students would gather in the schoolyard for ten minutes before the bell rang again, letting us know that it was time to return to our classrooms. It was an opportunity for us to get better acquainted and to make new friends.

After a few weeks, I had established a friendly relationship with a student in a class ahead of mine. He knew I was Jewish but didn't seem to care. So we gladly chatted about our mutual interests and occasionally went for walks along the canal Saint Martin not far from our school. As we were talking during one of these walks, he inadvertently mentioned that his uncle was Jewish. Then I understood why he was willing to befriend me, and why he was without prejudice toward Jews. Unfortunately, most of the other students were more reluctant to engage me in conversation for just this reason.

As a rule, our teachers were fair and considerate to all their students. They were not particularly influenced by the propaganda of the puppet government. This was especially true of our music teacher.

The music room of the college was built in the shape of an amphitheater or an old concert hall, and above the blackboard was a marble plaque dedicated to the composer Paul Dukas, who was an alumnus of College Turgot. After he had composed *L'apprenti sorcier* or 'The Sorcerer's Apprentice' in 1897, his reputation soared and he was now held in great esteem in his *alma mater*.

One day, as I was leaving the music room, my teacher asked me to wait, as he wanted to speak to me privately. He closed the door and pointed to the plaque above the blackboard, saying with a smile: "I am glad to let you know that the composer Paul Dukas who is mentioned on this plaque, was Jewish, like you."

Though we had never spoken to each other before, he must have known all along that I was Jewish, and although he was an organist at a nearby church and a devout Catholic, he had gone out of his way to tell me that a distinguished Jewish composer had also attended this class.

Just as Monsieur Marin, my primary school teacher had done the year before, my music teacher now felt the need to let me know—contrary to German and French official propaganda—that Jews had actually made valuable contributions to French culture. This encouragement from my teachers, combined with the positive reinforcement I received from my mother, enabled me to retain a sense of dignity and self-esteem through these difficult times.

After our classes were over in the afternoon, I would often walk to the municipal library and browse until I found one or two books related to what we were studying in school.* This was sometimes difficult, as I no

---

* The municipal library was situated next to the City Hall of the Third District of Paris.

longer wished to look through the children's books, but hadn't yet acquired enough vocabulary to understand many of the books in the adult section.

Our French literature teacher had encouraged us to broaden our vocabulary by looking-up words we didn't know in the dictionary, and I followed his advice. I made long lists of these words and studied them — together with the German words I now had to memorize for my classes — during my rides on the subway. This was a great help to me and I began to understand more and more of what I was reading in the adult section.

My mother also had a small library of her own at home. The books were arranged on two bookshelves in our living room. Browsing through them one day, I found an old prayer book in Hebrew with an inter-linear French translation which my mother must have used many times; for on many pages, there were clear impressions from her fingers or possibly from her tears. I immediately took it to my room and began to look through it. Soon it became one of my most treasured bedside books.

Every night, before falling asleep, I would read several pages from the Psalms, trying to imagine I was King David engaged in a dialogue with God. Within a few months, I knew two or three psalms almost by heart and recited them as I walked to school in the morning and back home in the late afternoon. Whenever I was overcome by fear, I would recite a verse from these psalms and feel comforted that God was watching over me and all his creatures. And when I went to bed each night, I asked God for guidance, to let me know what I should do about all the things that worried me. In this way I found the peace of mind I needed to fall asleep.

It was not always easy to tell the people I could trust

from the ones I should fear. Most people in France strongly resented the presence of the German troops on French soil, but there were others who seemed almost to approve of it. There was even a young man on our street who joined the pro-Nazi militia. He would come to visit his parents from time to time dressed in a black uniform, and whenever I saw him coming, I would run home as fast as I could.

According to our neighbors, he had been an extremely shy teenager before joining the militia. His parents were decent people who didn't like the Germans any more than the rest of us, but they were unable to dissuade their son from joining the militia. He had already been indoctrinated with its ideology and the uniform had given him the self-confidence and status for which he had so clearly longed.

In contrast, another young man who lived on our street had made a different decision. He had joined the Underground and was fighting the Germans in some remote, mountainous part of the country. We knew he was doing this, but we did not see him again until the liberation of Paris. He was careful not to come into the neighborhood as someone might have recognized him and denounced him to the police.

We had a suspicion that a certain widower who lived at the end of our street and who walked his dog every day might have been a spy or a collaborator reporting on any unusual movement in our neighborhood to the authorities.

Around this time, many Jews left their homes and all that they possessed, seeking refuge in other parts of the country. Some of them crossed the border between the German-occupied north of France and the southern part which had remained officially 'free,' being under the rule of the collaborationist government of Field Marshal Phillipe Pétain, who had been a hero of the French army during World War I.

If you had the money, you could avail yourself of the services of a *passeur*, a person who would help you cross the border where there was little police surveillance. But what these people who had fled to the 'free zone' did not know was that the police were keeping an eye on them. In time, they too were arrested and sent to concentration camps. Foreign Jews—especially the German and Austrian refugees who had arrived before the war had broken out—were the first to be apprehended. The conditions of their detention were harsh and many died from lack of medical care and proper nourishment.

The newspapers and radio announcers encouraged us to accept the legitimacy of the Pétain government installed in the resort city of Vichy. At school, our music teacher was forced to begin class with the newly composed patriotic song, *Maréchal, nous voila, le Sauveur de la France*—'Marshall, here we are, Savior of France.' While some students sang the words of the official version, others sang a satirical version introduced by one of our classmates. As there were almost forty students in the class, our teacher never realized what many of us were actually singing.

With respect to the national anthem, the *Marseillaise*, the authorities decided that we should only sing the second verse of the poem.[*] The first verse— which had been sung at all patriotic ceremonies for over 140 years—was deemed unflattering to the Germans. Indeed, it contained a reference to the villainy of the enemies of our nation (the Germans) who had invaded

---

[*] Written by poet and composer, Rouget de Lisle, at the beginning of the 19·century.

France in the aftermath of the French Revolution. Our teacher never explained to us why the national anthem had been changed . . . but our parents did.

The study of the German language was made compulsory immediately after the Nazis occupied France. Of course, they had two 'good' reasons for making it compulsory: the Nazis thought it was the finest language in the world, and they thought it would help the vanquished French adjust to their rule. Personally, I had my own reasons for wanting to study German: I had discovered that the language my grandparents spoke at home, Yiddish, was actually derived from medieval German!

Millions of Jews in Poland and Russia had been speaking this language ever since they were expelled from Germany in the 14th century in the aftermath of the epidemics of the Black Death. Acquainted with some of its basic vocabulary from my conversations with my grandmother, I was able to progress rapidly in the study of modern German, and at the same time, to learn more about the vocabulary and grammar of Yiddish.

For this class, we used a textbook which had been published before the war, and which contained a chapter devoted to the writings of the illustrious poet and writer, Heinrich Heine. After we had finished studying this section and memorized a few of his poems, our teacher passed around pairs of scissors and instructed us to cut the pages we had just studied from our book. He then collected them, placed them in a large envelope, and casually mentioned the fact that the Ministry of Education had requested that we remove these pages because they contained "a few mistakes."

When I told my mother what had happened in school, she told me that the poet Heine was Jewish and the Nazis had probably prohibited the study of his writings. In defiance of official instructions, however, our teacher had waited until *after* we had completed the study of that section before asking us to tear out the pages.

Whenever they wished to mark a victory on the Russian front, or celebrate the Führer's birthday, the Nazis would order a detachment of German soldiers to march in the main avenues of Paris singing military songs with a military band. The band was usually preceded by soldiers on motorcycles who made sure that no one was blocking the road. Whenever I heard the fanfare, I would duck into the corridor of a building in order not to be seen. I was afraid of what might happen if they spotted a Jewish boy standing on the sidewalk; for these parades were obviously meant to intimidate the French people and to remind us of German power and superiority.

Fearing that someone might overhear our conversation and realize we were Jews, my mother never uttered the word 'Jew' in public. If we were in the subway or on a train, she used a code word instead.

Once she said to me, "You see the people sitting on the next bench, Leo? I can assure you that they are both Eskimos."

Of course, I knew this was the code word. And when we got up to leave a little while later, I noticed that my mother winked at them while otherwise pretending not to know them.

When I asked her why she used the word, 'Eskimo,' she gave me the following explanation:

"Because Eskimos always recognize each other, and when they meet, they rub noses without saying a word. Now we have to do the same thing here in France. We glance at each other, and we know immediately whether they are alright or not, and whether we should be worried about some danger ahead. We are able to communicate all of this in the blink of an eye."

"So I'm an Eskimo too!" I said to my mother. "I will remember the secret."

Occasionally, my mother would say, "The pavement is slippery; let's take another road home." This meant that someone coming from the other direction had warned us with a look or a gesture that there was a checkpoint ahead and that the police were asking people to show their identity papers. In order to avoid this, we would turn aside at the first little street that presented itself and continue walking home as quickly as possible.

In time, we became quite good at this game of 'cat and mouse.' Sometimes, in order to meet their quotas, the police would spread their net in a given neighborhood and arrest anyone they suspected of some irregularity. Thus, we learned to keep a low profile and to walk in the street without being noticed, almost as if we didn't exist.

When we felt assured of someone's character or political stance, and that they wouldn't denounce us, we did not hesitate to share our feelings about the Germans and their puppet government. I remember the owner of the little grocery store near our home was one of these people. When we were the only customers in the shop, he would speak to us openly and without reserve. And when there was no food left on the shelves, he would bring out a few potatoes and carrots from the backroom which we gratefully bought from him.

Even though he Germans claimed that they were not 'occupying' France—only 'liberating' it from the Jews and other undesirables who controlled it—most people were not fooled, and in their private conversations, referred to them as the *boches* or *salauds,* 'cabbage-heads' or 'bastards.' No matter what they did to change their image, the fact remained that they had invaded our country, forced their rule upon us and persecuted our people.

Despite the danger, my mother and grandmother, my brother and I, all went to the synagogue on Rue Notre Dame de Nazareth in order to attend the Kol Nidre evening service on Yom Kippur, the most solemn holiday of the Jewish year. The synagogue was full, as Jews who had not attended a religious service in years now felt the need to gather in prayer with their brethren. The children were invited to sit on benches on both sides of the pulpit and I was pleased to be among so many other Jewish children.

The atmosphere was filled with emotion and sadness. The cantor sang beautifully and the rabbi gave a sermon in which he asked us to be resilient and to continue to trust in Providence in spite of the terrible hardships we had to endure. Thus, we returned home with a sense of peace in our hearts.

The next morning, however, when we went back to the synagogue to observe the Day of Atonement, we were profoundly distressed by what we saw. The front of the building had been destroyed in the night. Someone had planted a bomb under a seat in the synagogue the night before. We looked in horror on the ruins of the place where, only a few hours before, we had felt such peace. Desolate, we turned and went back home. Later we learned that seven synagogues had been bombed that night at the order of the German commander in charge of Jewish affairs.

Even in the face of such acts, my mother thought I should be formally initiated into the teachings of our faith. She registered me at the only religious school still functioning in the heart of Paris, Rue des Tournelles, near the Place de la Bastille. There were just a handful of students, and the classes were held in the back of the building which faced the Place des Vosges, one of the most beautiful squares of Paris, created in the days of the kings of France.

Our teacher, Monsieur Spector, wore thick glasses and a dark tie. He would present every lesson with great care and always thoroughly explained the meaning of the texts we were studying. In his class, I learned some of the fundamental principles of Judaism for the first time—the Ten Commandments, Maimonides' Thirteen Principles of Faith, and the significance of the holidays and prayers.

We also had a few sessions on comparative religion, which were quite enlightening to me. I learned with great surprise that Jesus of Nazareth was born of Jewish parents, and that he had lived and died as a Jew and had never renounced his allegiance to the Jewish religion!

"In spite of these explicit statements recorded in the New Testament," our teacher said in one of his lessons, "there are many people who believe in a Jewish Savior, but have difficulties accepting Jews as their neighbors." And he added with mild sarcasm, "If Jesus were living today, he might be arrested by the French police and deported to a concentration camp. Does that make any sense?"

On another occasion, Monsieur Spector said to us: "The biblical Prophets and the Talmudic Sages predicted long ago that when the Messiah comes, he will establish peace on earth and goodwill among the nations. The Sage Maimonides added: *'And though he may tarry, we must continue to hope and pray for his coming.'* So we must be patient until such a blessed time will come."

Looking back, I don't think he was a simple teacher at all, but more than likely, a university professor forced out of his position by the Nazis.

After several of the students were arrested with their families, the class was discontinued. I did not attend another Sunday school class or another synagogue service until after the war was over. I do not know what happened to Monsieur Spector, but I am reminded of him each time I speak of the things he taught me.

V

In the Face of Adversity

THE ALLIED FORCES' AIR RAIDS took place at night, and only rarely in the light of day. Quickly, the German anti-aircraft artillery would intervene, attempting to destroy the American or British planes in the air; but they were seldom successful. Likewise, the American bombers often missed their military targets, causing many civilian casualties.

Once, a bomb—probably meant to destroy a railroad dispatch center in Romainville—landed five miles away in Bagnolet. The next morning, the mayor and the fire chief came out to inspect the crater left by the bomb and found that the shell had not yet detonated! Without warning, it exploded, and a piece of shrapnel severed the mayor's head. The entire day, they searched the neighborhood until finally, they found the mayor's head in a garden about a hundred feet away.

Many people had gathered at the scene to see the hole left by the explosion, but instead, saw with horror the mayor's headless body covered with blood and lying on the ground. The sight was so gruesome and heartbreaking that no one uttered a word. We watched in silence, waiting for an ambulance to collect the body. For months afterward, I had recurring nightmares.

Occasionally, as we studied in our classrooms at school, the sirens would start to wail, announcing an air raid. The moment we heard the sirens, our teacher stopped class and conducted us to a bomb shelter in the basement of the school, where we were joined by people from the neighborhood. While we waited for the 'all-clear,' we quietly continued our lesson. And when the sirens went off a second time, we knew the air raid was over and returned to our classrooms and our studies as if we had just taken a break.

At home, there was no bomb shelter. When we heard the sirens, we sought refuge in the entrance corridor of our building, which opened toward the inner courtyard. From there we could see what was happening in the night sky. Often, the entire sky was illuminated by the flares which both sides used to get a better view of their targets. It was an awesome spectacle, like a scene of the creation of the universe.

Only in the light of day would we know whether the target aimed at by the Allied bombers had been destroyed, or whether the German anti-aircraft artillery had succeeded in destroying an American or British plane. Obviously, we could not rely on official reports to learn what had happened. So if we couldn't see for ourselves, we had to wait for the rumors to filter down to us.

Everyone knew that the official reports published in the newspapers and the broadcasts on the national radio were edited by government censors and supervised by the German High Command. As a rule, the news was only of German victories and never spoke of the Allies, except to ridicule the American and the British Air Force for their inability to carry out an effective military attack. Even after they began to retreat on the North African and the Russian fronts, the Germans continued to conceal the truth in this way.

On the other hand, we were fed a menu of news pertaining to another war directed against the most dangerous "parasites" of Europe—namely the Jews, Gypsies and Communists—who were undermining Western civilization. Jews were labeled, paradoxically enough, the most vicious "Communists" and the most corrupt "Capitalists" at the same time.

As I didn't really understand what these words meant, I went to the library to look them up. I wondered whether we were Capitalist, Communist, or both. Looking in the *Larousse Encyclopédique,* I found that Capitalism and Communism were opposites and mutually exclusive. We could either be one or the other, but hardly both at the same time. On further reflection, I came to the conclusion that my family couldn't have been either, for the simple reason that we did not possess any capital and no one in my mother's family had ever joined the Communist Party.

While I was reading a long essay in the encyclopedia, the librarian came by and offered to help me in my research. I told her I wanted to know whether it was possible to be a Capitalist and a Communist at the same time. She smiled and asked me kindly, "In what context are you asking this question?"

"On the radio, they say that Jews are all 'dirty Communists,' but at other times, they say that they are 'ruthless Capitalists'—I want to know which one of those statements is correct."

"Oh," she said, "you shouldn't pay too much attention to what broadcasters say in their official reports; they are often mistaken."

"Madame," I said, "I hear these things repeated again and again whenever I turn on the radio; do you mean to say that it isn't true?"

"These commentators often use fallacious arguments in order to manipulate public opinion. But for practical purposes, you should know that the Communists in the

Soviet Union are trying to establish a new society which requires that they destroy the capitalist economy. So you see, Capitalism and Communism do not go well together. But, tell me, young man, why are you so concerned about this question—Are you Jewish?"

"Yes, Madame, I am Jewish; and that's why it is important to me to understand what they say about my family."

Then she said, conspiratorially, "I will confess to you, young man, that I too am Jewish, but no one knows this. It is a secret and I hope you will keep it and not disclose it to anyone else."

"Promised," I said, "I am pleased to know that I now have a friend in the library."

"What is your name?" she asked.

"Leo Abramowski is my full name."

"And my name is Mireille Soleure, but it used to be Miriam Soloveitchick." And she quickly added, "This is *confidential* information, and it is important that no one should ever know my former name."

I responded, "*Enchanté*, Madame, I am delighted to know you."

"And me too, dear Leo.

"What I am going to tell you now may astonish you. My best friend, Suzanne, and her husband, Charles, who live in the same building, were arrested by the police two months ago. The moment I saw the policemen taking them away to their patrol car, I immediately went to the school to pick up their son Alain before the police found him. He was just coming out of school when I arrived, and I asked him to come with me.

"While we were walking, I told him what happened

48

and promised him that I would take care of him, as if he were my own son, until his parents returned. Since then, he has been living secretly with us. No one in the building must know that he is there and, as a consequence, he cannot leave the apartment unless we go out in the middle of the night. I would therefore appreciate your kindness if you were to visit him from time to time. Alain is just a year younger than you. I am leaving it to you to decide."

"Of course, I will," I responded, "but I will not have much time today, because I must go home soon. If I don't come back on time, my grandmother gets worried. But next Thursday, I will have more time."

"My shift will be over in fifteen minutes," said Mireille, "I will take you to my home, which is just two blocks away, and you will get acquainted with Alain. He will be so happy to see you!"

Shortly thereafter, Mireille and I walked to her apartment. She opened the door to let me in and then locked it behind us. She then went to Alain's room, knocked in an agreed upon code, and he immediately opened the door. We all went into the living room, where Mireille pulled the curtains and introduced us.

At first, Alain was afraid to talk; but when he realized that I was friendly, he began loosen up. I told him that I just wanted to greet him and promised that I would be back on Thursday when we could spend an hour together. In order to justify my presence in the building, we came up with a cover story. Mireille would let the neighbors know that I was coming to have a private lesson in French composition; for they all knew that Mireille had earned a master's degree in French literature, in addition to a diploma in library science.

So I came for my "lesson" the following Thursday and spent an hour with Alain, who was glad to see me, although still very sad on account of his separation from his parents. He didn't understand why it had happened, really, and I told him that he wasn't alone, that all the Jews of France were being persecuted in one way or another and that my mother and I barely escaped on several occasions. I also told him that he was fortunate to have two wonderful guardians providing a safe and warm home for him during this terrible period.

We also talked of school and he showed me the few schoolbooks he was carrying in his satchel the day his parents were arrested. I agreed to help him finish the books, and with Mireille's help, he would be able to keep up with his studies. She, of course, could borrow as many books as necessary from the library to keep him busy during the day until either she or her husband returned from work.

On my next visit, Alain asked me the same question I had asked myself only a year before—"Can you tell me," he said quietly, "what a Jew is?"

"You know, Alain," I said, "I found out myself only last year. I think I am clear about it now: Jews are a people like the Alsatians or the Normans, they just happened to have had a long history going back to antiquity. They existed before the Greek and the Roman empires came into being. Their sages conceived the basic principles of morality and religion, and they wrote their teachings in a unique book called the Bible. Moses, one of our great teachers, had proclaimed the unity of God and declared that we must love and respect our neighbor as ourselves."

I had barely learned these notions myself and here I was sharing them with a lonely boy whose parents had been brutally taken away from him because they were Jewish.

On another visit, Alain asked me a question I could

not answer: "Do you think my parents will ever come back?"

"I hope they will," I said, "but I confess that I don't know what the Nazis and their collaborators have against us, and why they are so mean to us."

"What should we do, then?" he asked.

I answered him the way my mother had when I asked her the same question. "This terrible war will eventually come to an end. We just have to be extremely careful and do everything we can to avoid being caught by the police for any reason, and we must pray that God will protect us from our enemies."

He was listening quietly, but I don't think he was convinced. He was still mourning the loss of his parents and was afraid he might never see them again. I couldn't even play a game with him. Nothing would alleviate his sadness and Mireille looked for a better way of helping him.

We listened to the radio every day hoping to hear good news, but it was all propaganda. We were bombarded with lies and misinformation devised by Joseph Goebbels, Adolph Hitler's Minister of Propaganda. We were urged to believe that the Aryan nation (i.e., the German people) constituted a superior race and that all other nations had an obligation to respect their ascendancy. At the bottom of their societal pyramid were the inferior races—Jews, Gypsies, and various other groups, like Communists and homosexuals—who had been declared a nuisance to humanity. Therefore, the Nazis were to be praised for having undertaken the unpleasant task of cleansing the earth of these societal misfits.

The radio announcers repeated these slogans again

and again until a segment of the French population actually came to believe them.

Many of our neighbors in Bagnolet were in fact members of the Communist party but hiding their affiliation, just as some Jews were concealing their Jewish-ness. But in the street, their children openly sang the International Socialist anthem—*C'est la lutte finale*—"This is the final struggle. Let us join together and tomorrow the *Internationale* will be the human race." I learned this song from my friends and knew it by heart, even before I learned the *Marseillaise,* the French national anthem.

Even though the authorities had strictly forbidden people to sing the Communist anthem, members of the Communist party defied the authorities and sang it at the end of all their gatherings. They had the advantage of being in the majority in Bagnolet, and many members of the police force were also sympathetic to Communist ideology.

Nevertheless, the fear of the *gendarmes,* the branch of the military serving as a civilian police force, was constantly hovering over our heads. We had to be vigilant and ready to activate our escape plan at any time. It usually involved a place where we could hide for a few hours and another where we could stay for a day or two if that were necessary. At such times, one rule took precedence over all the others; we called it "the eleventh commandment"—*"Thou shalt not get caught"*—for very few people were ever released after being questioned by the *gendarmes.*

As long as the Germans controlled most of Europe, they were in a position to assert the superiority of their race and the invincibility of their army. When it became known, however, that they had finally lost Stalingrad, the myth of the German superiority began to crumble and the Nazi dream of world domination began to seem like just so much smoke.

My mother and I were convinced that the war would soon come to an end, but unfortunately, the Vichy government wasn't and continued to arrest the Jews of France, sending them in cattle cars to the East. Nevertheless, this new conviction strengthened our determination to fight for our survival. I no longer paid much attention to the insults of my classmates because I believed that the victory of the Allies would bring about a new era of peace in Europe. I was also fortunate to have teachers who refused to endorse the official stand of the government and who encouraged me to pursue my studies without acknowledging the Nazi propaganda. As a result, I continued to do well in school and got good grades in all my subjects, except gymnastics and other athletic activities, in which I was not allowed to participate.

As swimming was a part of the sixth grade program, on the day of our first lesson, I went with my class to the public swimming pool. But our instructor soon took me aside and kindly reminded me that Jews were not permitted to enter a public sports arena, including the swimming pool. So I had to walk back to the college and wait for my classmates to return from the municipal pool.

In my history class, we studied ancient civilizations, which included the countries of the Fertile Crescent, often considered the cradle of civilization. Our textbook contained a whole chapter on the history of the Hebrews and their struggle to retain a national identity. We learned how this small nation was successively conquered by the Assyrians, the Babylonians, the Greeks and the Romans, who destroyed Jerusalem and called it *Aelia Capitolina*, "the city of the wind." It also told of how hundreds of thousands of Judeans had been taken captive by the Romans and sold as slaves. There was only one mention in the chapter that the Hebrews and Judeans followed the precepts of the Jewish religion. When our teacher spoke of this, I asked, "Teacher, may I ask a question? Was their religion the same as the one Jews follow today in various parts of the world?"

He answered: "Certainly. It is the same religion, because European Jews are the direct descendants of the Hebrews of biblical days and the Judeans who were eventually vanquished by the Romans."

"Teacher," I asked, "do we know what happened to the Judean captives who were sold as slaves in many parts of the Roman Empire?"

"They were most likely able to emancipate themselves after some time and most of them became Roman citizens. They were then allowed to settle in all the countries of the empire where they have lived for the past two thousand years.

"They were often expelled from one country after another and welcomed in another, and at other times invited to return to their original country. After several expulsions, which were later rescinded, the Jews of France were finally expelled from the country by Charles VI in 1394. Their descendants were allowed to return only in the years which followed the French Revolution, some four hundred years later."

More than once, I thought of escaping from this country whose government could not tolerate my presence. I thought of slipping away and going into hiding in some imaginary retreat, far away, waiting for the dawn of a new era.

One day, after I was spat on, I made plans to go away on my bicycle. I wasn't sure where I would go, but I packed some clothes, a flashlight, a camping knife, a map of France and my little prayer book in a bag, and I waited for some mysterious signal to let me know that it was time to escape. The signal never came and my plan was never realized.

The food rationing was severe and we were always looking for additional food to supplement our meager rations. During the summer months, we were fortunate in that we could barter the pears from our orchard for bread and cheese, but during the winter months, we had nothing to barter with and felt it keenly.

As my brother and I began to suffer from severe malnutrition, mother started to investigate new possibilities for finding the extra food we needed. She decided to visit an old acquaintance who had moved away from Paris and who had settled in the city of Laval, in Normandy, where she owned a grocery store. She was hoping that she might sell us some food without ration coupons.

We were aware of the enormous risk this would entail, for it was strictly forbidden for Jews to travel outside of the city without a permit, and such favors were usually refused. Nevertheless, my mother went to the railroad station of Gare Montparnasse and bought train tickets. We took the train bound for Brest and got off at Laval, a few stops after Le Mans, and went to the address of the grocery store. We were disappointed to find that there was little merchandise in the store. The owner was unable to sell us any food without rationing coupons, but she did give us some good advice: "You should go to the countryside" she said, "and try to find a farmer willing to sell you some food."

And that's precisely what my mother did. We went back to the train station, took an omnibus train this time, and got off at Evron, a little town twenty miles east of Laval. We asked a bus driver if his itinerary led to a farming community. He nodded in the affirmative and we got on the bus and went to the end of the line. We then walked for 15 or 20 minutes until we arrived at a farm.

We saluted the farmer's wife as she was feeding the rabbits in their cage, and my mother asked her if she would sell us a chicken or some eggs. After a short conversation, during which she said that it was forbidden by law to do so, she agreed to sell us two-dozen eggs. We thanked her and continued our walk along a little path which was wide enough to allow a horse and a narrow cart to pass. There were rows of trees and bushes on both sides. We visited a few more farms and succeeded in filling our three bags with food.

The farmers were reluctant to sell us anything for fear of being denounced, but my mother would insist that it was not for herself, but for her children that she needed that extra food, and many would set aside the rule and sell us some of their farm products.

In due course, my mother learned her way and became quite skilled in the art of bartering clothes for food. Rather than ask a favor, she was now doing business with the farmers; she would take orders and promise to endeavor to find the clothes, the batteries or the medicines they needed for their family, and bring the items in exchange for food. As a consequence, the farmers were now looking forward to my mother's visits to get what they could not find in their villages, and thus she obtained the food we needed.

My mother would make a trip to the country every four or five weeks and took my brother or me with her to help carry the packages. We would take the buses that served the area and walk long distances from the bus stops to the farms, unless a friendly motorist or a farmer with horse and cart offered us a ride to our destination.

On one of these journeys, my mother and I arrived at a farm in the late afternoon, and before we could even talk to anyone, we saw the farmer seated with his arm on a table in great discomfort. He was suffering from a swelling in his right hand that had obliged him to abandon the team which was busy harvesting the wheat in the fields. When my mother saw his hand, she said, "Monsieur, you should soak your hand in a basin filled with warm water."

Immediately, the farmer's wife brought out an old bowl which was not very clean and put some water in a pot over the fireplace to boil the water. When my mother saw the bowl, she said, "Wait a minute, Madame, we have to sterilize this bowl." She cleaned it as well as she could and said to the farmer's wife, "Can you bring me a little glass of *gnaule* (apple brandy)?"

After the farmer's wife brought the brandy, my mother poured it in the bowl and struck a match which caused a fire to burn for a few seconds. By now, the water was boiling and she poured it in the bowl and brought it to the farmer, saying: "If you soak your hand in the warm water every two hours, the swelling and the pain may go away. If it doesn't, you should go to the doctor at the first hour tomorrow morning, for this is probably an abscess and the doctor may have to make a small incision in order to disinfect the area of the infection."

Thus, my mother and I spent the night in the main room of the farm to assist the farmer. As the swelling did not subside, we all went to town the next morning and my mother accompanied the farmer to the infirmary. The doctor took a look at the swelling and immediately made his diagnosis: the swelling was most certainly caused by an abscess and he had to make an incision in order to clear up the infection. The farmer and his wife were absolutely amazed. They turned toward my mother and said: "Madame Léon, how did you know that the swelling had to be treated that way? Everything you said was confirmed by the doctor!"

My mother explained that she had been working as a social worker in a hospital, and that similar cases occurred frequently. She also knew that in all these cases, it is necessary to sterilize whatever comes into contact with the wound, and that is why she had requested brandy to sanitize the bowl, since there was no hydrogen peroxide or another antiseptic solution at the farm.

The doctor treated the farmer and he bandaged the hand to protect it from any further infection. He told the farmer that he should come back in a week so that he might change the dressing and make sure the wound was healing properly. The farmer and his wife went back to the farm, but just before he left us, he suggested that we pay a visit to one of his cousins who owned a grocery store in town. He even said, "Please tell him that I sent you to him, and I am sure he will be nice to you and sell you the food you need."

Mother did exactly as he suggested and we went back to Paris with enough food to last us another month.

Our triumph was soon overshadowed by the realities of life in Paris. When we arrived at the Gare Montparnasse, we saw that the police had established checkpoints at the four exits of the railroad station. There was simply no way to get out of the station without first going through a police inspection. They were asking every traveler to show identification and searching every bag and suitcase. Had we gone forward, we would surely have been caught in their net. My mother quickly analyzed the situation and came up with the only escape route available to us short of a miracle.

Instead of trying to leave the station by one of the gates, she decided to find a train that was about to depart. She looked on the main board and saw there was a train leaving for Versailles. We hurried toward the departure platform and mother quickly told the conductor that she didn't have time to buy a ticket at the window because we were late and afraid of missing the train.

The conductor merely smiled and assured her, "That's alright, lady, we'll wait another twenty seconds until you get aboard."

Once we were on board, we bought tickets from the controller who came to our compartment. We told him that we had not been able to purchase them earlier because we were in a rush to catch the train. He told us that the conductor had already informed him of the situation and he waived the fine that he would normally have charged. Less than half an hour later we were in Versailles.

We left our luggage at the baggage room and spent a few hours walking in the vicinity of the railroad station in Versailles. Unexpectedly finding myself in the City of the Kings, I told my mother that this might be a perfect opportunity for visiting the Chateau. But she said: "Leo, there will be other opportunities I hope to visit the famous Chateau de Versailles, but at this very moment, we are only trying to avoid being caught by the police. Be patient, and when the war is over, we'll come back and visit as tourists do."

After this impromptu excursion, we caught another train back to Paris and tried our luck again. This time, when we got off the train, the checkpoints were gone. We were thus able to leave the station and take the subway home without having to confront the police.

As we arrived home much later than we had planned, we found my grandmother and brother waiting anxiously. My mother only said that the train was delayed.

Obviously, there was no need for children like myself to play cops and robbers at school or camp. It was a game my mother and I played each time we went out of the house. Whenever we were faced with one of these situations, we had only seconds to come up with a plan to avoid being caught. And having escaped the threat, we always experienced a feeling of relief and satisfaction. Thus, we expressed our gratitude to the Master of our Destinies for having saved us once more from the beast who hunted us.

I went back to school the next day and said nothing of my adventure to anyone. But I was proud of my mother's quick thinking and found myself reliving the whole episode again and again in my thoughts. This is what I was doing when a classmate, with whom I had never spoken before, approached me during the break.

"My name is Claude," he said, "and I know you are Jewish. I have something to tell you that may be of interest to you and your family. But you must promise to be very discreet, and not to let anyone know what I am going to tell you."

"I promise," I said, "I won't tell anyone except my mother."

"Fine," said Claude, "I want you to know that my father is involved in the rescue of people who have problems with the police, such as Jews and Communists. My father and his friends are manning a few safe houses in Paris and they help people in danger of being arrested to get into the 'free zone,' and even to cross the border into Spain. If your family needs this kind of assistance, I will introduce you to my father; but remember, no one else is to know about our conversation."

So I told my mother about Claude's offer, but her reaction was one of caution.

"Beware, Leo" she said, "there are unscrupulous people out there extorting money from people like us, promising them all kinds of services; but once they have the money, they do not fulfill their promises, and in some cases, they even denounce them to the police."

"I understand—I will be careful." The next day, during the break, Claude approached me again and asked, "Did you have a chance to talk to your parents? Are they interested in getting to the free zone?"

"Possibly," I said "but not at this moment. We may be interested in the coming weeks or months."

"In that case," he said, "I think you should meet my father. Let's pick a day and after school we can walk to my house. How about tomorrow?"

"Alright," I said, "it's a deal."

The next day, we walked a mile to his house and he introduced me to his parents. They seemed to be fine people, but my mother had warned me to be extremely cautious and I was on my guard.

His father welcomed me and said: "I know what it means to be on the black list of the police. You Jews, you have known that predicament for some time. That's why I would like to tell your folks that I could help you cross the border whenever you want to do so. Please tell your mother that my friends and I can arrange this whenever you decide."

"Is there a fee for such a service?" I asked

"Yes, there is," he said, "we are asking three

thousand *francs* per person – but everything is negotiable."

"What if we don't have that much money?" I asked.

"Then," he said, "we will accept jewelry or antiques instead of the money. You see, there is a lot of risk involved for us too, and we have to be compensated for it."

"How dangerous is the crossing?"

"When you are dealing with the German and the French police forces combined, there is always great danger. Our task is not an easy one: to help people pass the border without being caught requires that we be extremely well informed about the terrain and the police patrolling in the area."

I didn't pursue the subject any further because I wasn't sure whether to trust him or not. I said I would let my mother know about his offer and convey her answer to Claude as soon as she gave me one.

The next day, Claude came up to me during the morning break and said that his father wanted to talk to my mother, as he had some important news to share with her. My mother agreed to a brief meeting the next day, using the pretext of picking me up from school as an excuse. That afternoon, my mother came to fetch me and I introduced her to Claude's father. They whispered together, and he told her that it was becoming more and more difficult to cross the border. His friends were not sure how long they would be able to help people get to the other side. My mother thanked him for his kindness and told him that she would contact him when she was ready to make the move.

After we took leave of Claude and his father, my mother told me: "Leo, I have heard several stories about these *passeurs* (guides), who supposedly help you pass from one side of the border to the other, at some place where there is little or no police surveillance. Many Jews are desperate and ready to pay whatever fee these people demand. And most *passeurs* are probably honest people, but there are also some 'sharks' among them. They have found a way of helping others and *themselves* at the same time."

We never availed ourselves of the service which Claude's father offered us because our first plan of escape was to flee to Normandy where we had established many friendly contacts with good people.

We returned to Evron a few weeks later. We took the usual bus to the last stop and walked fifteen minutes until we arrived at the first farm. There, mother was greeted by the farmer's wife, who immediately invited us to have lunch with her and her daughters. She showed her the dress she had brought her from Paris and the farmer's wife was very pleased with it. She was thus able to barter it for two chickens and three-dozen eggs.

We then continued our visits and walked to the next farm where we intended to deliver some men's clothes in exchange for more farm products. When we entered the living room, we found the farmer's wife very concerned about her daughter's health. She was suffering from severe pain in her abdomen and the farmer couldn't go to the city for a doctor. My mother asked a few questions of the girl and quickly realized that she was suffering from severe constipation. Then she said: "It just so happens that I have a vial of *senna* pills in my purse. I assure you, if your daughter takes two or three of them tonight, she will be relieved in the morning."

Thus, we spent the night in the barn, and the next morning, at dawn, when we met the whole family for breakfast, the daughter was smiling again. She thanked my mother and asked if she could have the rest of the magic pills in the vial. The farmer and his wife were also grateful and said to my mother: "Madame Léon, you need not walk to another farm to find additional provisions for your family; this time *we* will provide you with all you need."

In this way, my mother gained a good reputation that quickly made its way around the village and the nearby farms. She no longer had any problem convincing the farmers to sell her food. They were all glad to welcome her now and usually invited her to sit down to a meal with them. They would often ask her about health and family matters and always appreciated her common sense and practical answers. From time to time, they would even ask her for advice on business problems or legal matters. When she did not know the answer to one of these questions, she would tell them that she would inquire in the city and bring them the answer on her next visit.

By now, mother only needed to walk to two farms in order to obtain all the food we could carry without causing too much suspicion at the railroad station. The station was always the scariest part of our journey, because the police were often there, checking the identity cards and the luggage of virtually every traveler about to take a train. Somehow, mother always managed to get us through this dangerous situation. Once, she smiled at the policemen and showed them the head of a live chicken she was carrying in her bag and joked with them—"I don't have papers for this fellow!" The policemen laughed and let us go without checking our papers.

On her next visit, the mayor of the village let my mother know that he wanted to speak to her. Mother was apprehensive—afraid that someone might have denounced us for some reason—but we went anyway.

"Madame Léon," the mayor said, "I have heard many good things about you, and I want to tell you personally that I appreciate everything you are doing for our farmers. I am aware of the fact that we are in the middle of a war and that food rationing is a major problem for your family, so I would like to make a proposal to you: we have an empty house in the village; why don't you come and live with us in Sainte Gemmes le Robert? We'll do everything we can to make your stay as pleasant as it can be."

My mother thanked the mayor and told him that she would talk to her elderly mother and give him an answer on her next visit. But, as hard as she tried to convince my grandmother, she refused to move from her house in Bagnolet, saying: "The Germans don't need an old woman like me. What good would it be for them?"

As my mother could not resign herself to leaving grandmother alone in Paris, she informed the mayor on her next visit that she would not be able to accept his generous offer, but would continue to visit her friends in the area every four or five weeks.

On one of these journeys, however, we faced a very dangerous situation, which could have been disastrous for us. It happened as we were returning from our visit to the farms and walking in the direction of the railroad station of Evron in order to catch the last train to Paris. We had been walking a great deal that day and I was tired. I said to my mother, "I cannot carry these packages anymore; they are too heavy." I dropped them on the ground and stopped walking.

My mother knew that we could not be late for the train, because if we missed it, we would have to spend the night in a hotel, and the night clerk would require that my mother leave her identity card at the desk for the police inspection. Then they would find out that we were Jews traveling without a permit.

Realizing the gravity of the situation, my mother quickly looked around for help. She saw a German soldier standing in front of the window of a fashion store and approached him. She asked him if he would help us carry our packages to the railroad station. He agreed without hesitation and picked up all our bags and we all walked swiftly toward the station.

As we were approaching the station, however, the soldier saw that members of the *Gestapo* (German police) and the French police were asking all travelers to show their identity cards. At that moment, the soldier refused to go any further and whispered a few words of excuse to my mother. He put down the packages and quickly left. But my mother thanked him profusely, and loudly—*Danke Schoen, Mein Herr. Auf Wiedersehn!* "Thank you very much and goodbye!"—making sure that the German policemen could hear her. Then we picked up our bags and continued to the gate. As we appeared to be on friendly terms with a German soldier, the Gestapo let us pass without asking to see our papers; and when the French police saw that their counterparts did not stop us, they also let us go.

The train had just entered the station, the *chef de gare*, the stationmaster, helped us into our compartment and we soon departed for Paris.

My mother was pale and I was shivering from the close call. Our neighbors in the train compartment seemed concerned and offered us some water and a sandwich which my mother kindly refused. They continued to try and cheer us up, but we simply couldn't manage a conversation and mostly remained silent until we arrived in Paris.

Grandmother and my brother were waiting for us

again, but mother said nothing about the episode, not wanting to cause her mother any pain or worry.

Had the policemen asked to see my mother's papers, they would have seen the word *Juif* or 'Jew' stamped on her identity card, and would have known that we were breaking the law by traveling outside of our city of residence without a permit. We would have been arrested on the spot and most likely deported. But, as it happened, a German soldier saved our lives!

VI
The Means of Escape

MY MOTHER had heard that there were expert forgers among the members of the Underground capable of producing identity cards that were almost impossible to detect as forgeries. But for some reason, she hesitated in pursuing this option. Instead, she opted for another, perhaps less dangerous solution to protect her children. She went to see a Catholic priest who was known for his compassion and willingness to help people in danger and asked him to write baptismal certificates for me and my brother.

He kindly agreed to do so, and said to my mother: "These are provisional certificates. If, at any time in the future, you feel like making true the promise that they contain, I will be delighted to assist your children in becoming good Catholics."

"I understand, Father," said my mother, "and I thank you for extending your kindness to these two boys, who may be saved from deportation on account of the certificates you have just signed. We will consider *spiritual* salvation when the war is over."

From that day forward, I was instructed to tell people that my name was Michel Léon, and that I was a native of Laval. For this new identity, I even created a fictional ancestry connected with one of the knights of King Arthur's Round Table and memorized his story, just in case I was asked to prove this new identity!

When we returned to Normandy the following month, my mother decided to spend an hour in Evron before getting on the bus which took us to the countryside. She had been unable to find a pair of boots in Paris that one of the farmers had ordered from her, and in a last ditch effort to find the promised boots, she entered a shoe store and asked the owner if she had the size she needed.

The store's owner smiled and said: "These boots are worn by farmers and fishermen, not by city dwellers like you; why do you need such a pair of boots?"

My mother explained that it was not for her, that she wanted the boots but for a farmer who did not have the time to come to town to purchase them. It was part of an arrangement, whereby she would barter the boots for food in order to supplement the diet of her children and her aging mother. Madame Lemaître, the owner of the store was touched by my mother's explanation and asked for her name. My mother hesitated a moment before answering, "Madame Léon."

The storeowner must have understood immediately that we were among those who were harassed by the authorities and said: "Madame Léon, I will do everything I can to help you. First, I have the boots you are looking for and my assistant will bring them to you in a moment."

"This is very kind of you, Madame," said my mother. "In the future, I will come to you to buy all the shoes that my farmers order from me instead of looking for them in Paris."

Then the owner made us a very generous offer: "Madame Léon, if you ever need a place to stay when you come to our city, you can stay with me. I have a little room in the attic where there is a bed and you may spend the night there."

Thus, on one of our subsequent journeys to Evron, we availed ourselves of the offer and stayed in the attic room above the store. Madame Lemaître invited us to join her family in prayer before we sat down for dinner. After the meal, she told us that there were some good people in the city, who were "true Frenchmen," and that they might help us if we needed emergency assistance. She didn't say anything more on the subject, but we understood to what she was alluding. We had heard that there were Underground groups operating in the area, which was the reason why the Germans had intensified their vigilance in the region.

A month later, we heard that the offices of the civil registry had been broken into during the night and that many blank identity cards had been stolen, but that the head of the office had not reported this to the police. He only mentioned that a few typewriters had been stolen, but nothing else.

Even in a little town like Evron, the people were divided on the subject of the occupation, just as they were in Paris. Some were willing to collaborate with the government, while others were just trying to get by without getting into trouble. And there were still others, patriots and members of the armed resistance who strongly resented the presence of the German troops on French soil, and who were fighting them in every possible way. They sabotaged every undertaking of the enemy at every opportunity.

When we met new people, however, we had to be particularly cautious; we never knew what their allegiance might be, or whether they would denounce us to the police. The German command and the French police had devised a whole system of surveillance and monitoring of the population in order to maintain full control over them. We were required to report all suspicious activities and the names of the individuals involved in them. In addition, the police had hired informers who were to let them know about individuals who might be connected to the Underground, or Jews and Communists who might be hiding in the neighborhood. This system created a climate of suspicion and mistrust among the members of the community and sometimes even between the members of the same family.

On one of our next visits to Evron, we entered a pastry shop to buy some croissants, and said, "Bonjour." The owner, sitting behind the cash register, responded to our greeting and asked us what brought us to the city. Mother simply answered, "We have come to visit a cousin recovering from the flu."

"In that case, you are most welcome here. You know, Madame, there are people who come here from time to time in order to take advantage of us and we don't want them here," said the woman.

"What kind of people are you talking about?" asked my mother.

"The Jews; they're an unscrupulous and dishonest people. The Germans are right to take them away. They're sending them to work in Germany and that's what they deserve."

"Are there any Jews in Evron?" asked my mother in a relaxed manner.

"I don't know," said the pastry shop owner, "but I can assure you, if one showed up in my shop, I'd denounce him to the police at once. We have to get rid of those people; they're a plague in our midst."

"I would never have thought that Jews would come to Evron," said my mother. "I was told that they like to spend their money in the posh casinos of Deauville or Monte Carlo; why would they come to a peaceful little town like this one?"

"Madame, you don't know the Jews," said the owner, "they would go anywhere if they thought they could swindle some unsuspecting person. They are the worst Capitalists you can imagine, and others say that they are also mean Communists on top of it."

"Madame, I hope they will never enter your shop, and never have a chance to enjoy your delicious croissants," said my mother.

"Indeed, Madame," said the owner, "Have a nice visit with your cousin. I will be glad to see you when you return to our city . . . Madame?"

"Madame Leon," said my mother, "*Au revoir,* until we see you again."

We had learned to be actors and to pretend we were not who we were. We had come to understand that there was no sense in arguing with bigots like this woman who claimed to know everything about Jews though she had never met one in her life . . . *until that day!*

I admired my mother's amazing talent, being able to play different roles as the situation required. I knew that she strongly disapproved these forms of dissimulation, but survival often necessitated these exceptions she made.

When we arrived at the first farm that trip, we learned that the youngest son of the farmers had decided to join the Underground. He said goodbye to his parents one evening and left the farm without telling them how they could contact him.

The policeman in charge of security in the area heard about this sudden disappearance and came to question the farmer in order to send a report to his superiors. The farmer told him that he had no idea where his son had gone and that he would let him know if he heard from him. Of course, that was not the *entire* truth, but it was close enough. He then asked the police to let him know if they, in turn, had any information about his son.

My mother bartered a few pair of pants and a dress for all the food we needed and we returned to Evron. We stopped in the store of Madame Lemaître, who was pleased to see us, and told us with a smile that the police stationed at the railroad station were only checking the identity cards of men today and were letting the women go by without an identity check. My mother understood the message and decided to wait until the last minute before going to the station.

We continued our walk and briefly stopped at the pastry shop to buy croissants for the journey back to Paris. The owner asked us if our cousin had recovered from the flu. We said that he felt much better and didn't need our help anymore, and then we continued on our way to the station. As Madame Lemaître had said, the policemen did not ask for our papers and we boarded the next train to Paris.

We found two empty seats in the first compartment we checked and decided to take them. Two well-dressed gentlemen were sitting across from us and soon started a conversation with my mother who immediately realized that, even though they spoke a very good French, they were not natives of France. They kept referring to the French in the third person, using the pronoun "they." And when my mother gave me a book to read in order to keep me occupied, one of the men turned toward her, and for no apparent reason asked, *Madame, ce garçon atil été bap-tisé?* "Madame, has this boy been baptized?" But from the way he pronounced the word *"baptize,"* my mother understood that they were most likely Germans who spoke correct French, but not well enough to know that the letter *p* in *ba-p-tisé* is not pronounced in spoken French.

At once, my mother responded, "Of course, both of my sons were baptized when they were only a few months old."

The Germans seemed satisfied by her spontaneous answer. She did not bother to tell them that she even had a baptismal certificate to prove it! The man then turned to me and asked me in a sweet voice, "In what grade are you at school?"

"In the sixth grade," I answered.

Then he then asked me, "If you are a sixth grader, then tell me — have you already begun the study of German in your school?"

"Ja mein Herr," (Yes, sir) I responded, "we have already covered almost half of our textbook," and I began reciting a poem by Goethe.

"Das ist sehr gut!" (That is very good!) he said, and from this response in German, my mother concluded that the two men were, without a doubt, Nazi agents. She made no attempt to speak to them in German herself, as she might have inadvertently used a Yiddish word. However, she did manage to communicate to me by her looks that I was to be extremely careful in my conversation; the two men were not to be trusted. Fortunately, this casual conversation ended the moment we arrived in Paris.

When we returned to Bagnolet, my grandmother and brother were relieved to see that we were safe. They were well aware that these excursions to the country were sometimes like walks through a minefield.

After we had reassured them that all had gone well and shown them the provisions that would keep us going for another month, my grandmother told us what happened to the Schneiders, who lived just a few blocks from our house.

Samuel and Eva Schneider were both naturalized French citizens who had come to France from Russia. He was a tailor and she a seamstress. They had two children, who often walked to school with me in the morning.

When the authorities decreed that Jews could no longer be lawfully employed in any business or company, both had lost their jobs with a department store. Now they had only a few private customers who still availed themselves of their services and were barely making ends meet.

When the French government cancelled many of the naturalizations of former immigrants and the police increased their arrests in the neighborhood, the Schneiders feared for their lives and decided that the time had come for them to go into hiding. Since they didn't have enough savings to go away and find some retreat in the country, they asked their neighbor, Monsieur Dupont, if he were willing to let them live in the dilapidated little cottage which stood at the end of his property.

They assured him that they were ready to do anything necessary to keep anyone from suspecting that someone might be living in the cottage: they would not come out into the yard during the day; they would not use any light at night; and they would keep quiet all the time.

After discussing the matter with Monsieur Dupont, they came to an agreement whereby he would allow the Schneiders to live in the cottage and would provide them with food and, in exchange, the Schneiders agreed to work for him making suits and dresses. In order to further camouflage their hiding place, a chicken coop was installed just next to the entrance of the cottage.

Monsieur Dupont owned a clothing store across from the open market. He had always sold 'ready-made' clothes, but when this opportunity presented itself, he decided to expand his business to include a line of 'made-to-measure' suits and dresses which he would sell at a premium. He would let the customer choose the fabric they liked, he would take their measurements himself, and then would tell them that the suits or dresses that they had ordered would be ready in a week. Thus, Monsieur Dupont found a convenient way of helping his business and a Jewish family in distress at the same time.

It was not long before the police came to arrest the Schneiders at their former address. When no one answered the door, they called a locksmith to open the door and they searched the house; they found no one, the house had been deserted.

A few months went by in the cottage before the Schneiders had any real trouble. But one night, the tailor and his wife were awakened by a startling noise, followed by the loud clucking of the chickens right outside their door. It seemed a burglar was trying to steal some of the chickens from the coop! Immediately, the tailor yelled and the intruder ran off without a single chicken.

The problem was, it was now clear that someone was living in the cottage; and someone who had come to steal from them would certainly have no compunction about reporting them to the police for a reward. Thus, the tailor went to see Monsieur Dupont immediately. He told him what had happened and they agreed that it would be wise for the tailor and his family to leave the property at once, as the police might arrive at any time.

Where would the tailor and his family go in the middle of the night? After exploring several possibilities, the tailor decided to return with his family to their own home, next door, to enter by the back door and spend the rest of the night there. So they climbed over the fence into their own yard, opened the back door, and went straight to a bedroom in the dark, remaining as quiet as possible.

They had barely tucked their children in their beds when they heard a police car pull up in front of Monsieur Dupont's house. Two policemen got out of the car and knocked loudly at his door and demanded to speak to the owner of the cottage.

"Monsieur Dupont," they said, "we have orders to search your house and the little cottage on your property. We have reason to believe that someone is living in it."

"You must be mistaken, Gentlemen," said Monsieur Dupont, "I have never allowed anyone to live in the cottage . . . though, I suppose a transient may have broken in without my being aware of it. I have recently installed a chicken coop in front of it and, it's possible that some marauder may have tried to steal my chickens during the night! But please, see for yourselves?"

The two policemen went out to the cottage and inspected it thoroughly. All they found were some scraps of fabric on a table and a few old newspapers from the previous year; for the tailor and his wife had stuffed their clothes in a bag and wrapped their children in the blankets before abandoning the cottage. The policemen went back to Monsieur Dupont's house, looked perfunctorily in every room and then excused themselves for having disturbed him in the middle of the night.

The burglar who had reported that someone was living in the cottage received no reward.

The next day, Monsieur Dupont arranged for a friend to take the tailor and his family to a Summer house he owned in the country, some twenty miles from Paris. Samuel and Eva Schneider and their two children waited until nightfall before quietly entering the car of Monsieur Dupont's friend and leaving for the country.

After this, Monsieur Dupont visited them once or twice a week, bringing them food and fabric for the new orders his customers had placed, and to pick up the finished clothes from the previous week. In this way, the Schneiders survived the war. In time, Monsieur Dupont took them on as partners in his business.

My grandmother, who was a very religious woman, was convinced that the tailor and his wife must have had a great spiritual merit; this was the only explanation she could offer for why Providence had protected them and their children. After all, so many other people and children were not so fortunate. This was the circumstance that challenged the faith of everyone we knew at the time: why did some escape while others, who seemed equally innocent, were arrested and deported?

Everyday, we prayed with all our hearts for protection, but this alone, was not enough. We also had to be cunning enough to avoid being caught in the net of the police, and intrepid enough to survive and avoid starvation.

If the Schneiders had not acted quickly, and conceived of some means of escape ahead of time, they would not have been able to evade arrest and its terrible consequences. Of necessity, we had always to be one step ahead of the enemy. We had to play the game of cops and robbers with the utmost sincerity, though we did not know at the time, or simply refused to believe, that it was literally a matter of life and death. I was only ten years old and didn't really have the capacity to conceive of how terrible people could be to one another, but I was learning quickly.

Today, I wish I had been a few years older so that I might have helped to rescue others who were in danger.

VII
Living in Fear

IN EARLY JUNE OF 1942, arrests of Jews in Paris and its surrounding areas increased dramatically; for in May, the Nazis had appointed Louis Darquier de Pellepoix, a notorious anti-Semite, Commissioner for Jewish Affairs. And among his first acts was to set higher arrest quotas for Jews.

Sadly, the French police, in general, wasted no time in executing Darquier's orders; nevertheless, there were occasions on which a benevolent policeman might warn a few Jewish families in the middle of the night that they were to be arrested at dawn. Thus, they would immediately go into hiding, fleeing in the middle of the night without a word to anyone.

Some families made contingency plans for just such a possibility. In most cases, these plans included an immediate flight to an abandoned house or basement where they could spend a few hours before taking their escape route which usually led into seclusion somewhere in the countryside. But others simply closed their eyes and hoped that nothing would happen to them, especially if they did not break any of the regulations set by the authorities. Still, the handwriting was on the wall, and no matter how scrupulously one followed the rules, no Jew was safe from arrest. It was all about excuses. And there was always the possibility that some acquaintance, for whatever reason, might denounce you to the police. Sometimes, it was even for the purpose of being able to move into your apartment!

When my uncle Simon, my mother's brother, left Paris to seek refuge in the 'free zone' with his wife, Jeannette — in a village near Clermont-Ferrand — they asked my mother to watch over their apartment and their belongings. The concierge of the building had been instructed to give us the keys whenever we came on condition that we return them to her before we left.

When we came to air out the apartment and make sure that everything was in good order, we were pleased to discover a few cans of vegetables and some packages of noodles and rice in the pantry, which we took home with us. But when we came back sometime later, the concierge asked us to come into her apartment, as she wanted to talk to us. She spoke quietly, almost whispering, and we knew that she had something important to say.

"Madame Leon," she said, "I hope your brother and his wife are doing well wherever they are, but I must warn you that there is a tenant in this building who works as an informer for the police and who is reporting everything that is happening in the neighborhood. He must be the one who denounced the family living in the apartment on the fifth floor facing the garden.

"The Bernsteins were very quiet people and only came out of their apartment late at night, so that no one might suspect that they were actually living in the building. But the bastard must have seen them and reported them to the police! Consequently, they were all arrested last week and probably taken to the camp at Drancy. You must, therefore, be very careful when you come here, because if he finds out about you, he may denounce you too!"

With a sigh, my mother replied, "I am most grateful to you. I will act accordingly and not come back after today's visit. We will return the keys in a short while."

We checked the apartment quickly, locked the door, and went down the stairway. As we arrived in the lobby, on our way out of the building, a man approached us and said: "I have never seen you in the building before; did you find the person you were looking for?"

"Yes, Monsieur, I certainly did," my mother replied. "I just came by to say hello to an old friend."

"And how did you find him?" he asked.

"He was fine, thank you. My son and I must go home now; it's getting late, and I still have to run a few errands. *Au revoir, Monsieur.*"

The man did not attempt to continue this contrived conversation, which sounded more like an inquiry than a friendly exchange. We felt certain that he must be the informant the concierge had mentioned.

We immediately left him and walked quickly for a few minutes, crossing several streets and eventually mingling with a crowd of by-standers who had gathered in a square where a musician was playing the harmonica, a xylophone, and drums with a system of ropes attached to his feet. When my mother was certain we hadn't been followed, we quickly went down the stairs of an escalator and took the train home.

The man had obviously suspected us of hiding in the building and was trying to verify his suspicion in order to denounce us to the police, no doubt hoping for some reward. Though we were *not* hiding in the building, even a false accusation might have been enough to have us arrested and deported, especially if that police precinct had not yet met their quota of Jews for the week.

On the recommendation of one of the Jewish organizations still allowed to function in France, my mother soon took me to a kind of impromptu foster home, situated in little town, some 25 miles north of Paris.* She did this for my safety, thinking that I might be better protected there than in the city.

I was one of twelve Jewish boys and girls in the custody of Madame Jeanne. We slept in camp beds in an enclosed garage. There was only one bathroom for all of us, and we were not allowed to flush the toilet after each use. The meals were very simple and usually consisted of boiled potatoes and carrots with apples or pears for desert.

Madame Jeanne had made a few books and games available to us and we were allowed to read or play, as long as we didn't raise our voices. We had to keep quiet at all times, so as not to arouse the suspicion of the neighbors. For me, it seemed the nearest thing to being in prison.

After only three weeks, my mother returned to take us back to Paris. Madame Jeanne tried to convince her that we were safe in her custody, but my mother was adamant. She must have had a premonition about the fate of the children who were living in Madame Jeanne's foster home; for, the following week, we heard that the children were all arrested and deported to concentration camps.

My mother's instinct was usually right. She knew that the Union Générale des Israélites de France, which was supposed to assist the members of the Jewish community, was itself supervised by the Commissariat Général aux Questions Juives (Commission for Jewish Affairs), which, as we already have said, was under Nazi control. Thus, the efforts made by the organization to

---

* My brother was taken to a different foster home. His own story is more dramatic than mine, but until recently, he has refused to talk about it.

protect these children came to nothing, for the Germans and their French accomplices knew how to access the information whenever they needed it to meet their arrest quotas.

By the end of June, the Commissariat had ordered Jews to wear a yellow star with the word *Juif,* 'Jew,' printed in black (and resembling the shape of Hebrew letters) on the left side of their garments. We were now singled out like criminals. Our ethnic and religious identity, already indicated by a stamp on our identity cards, was now written in big letters on the stars we were compelled to wear at all times. Those who refused to comply were arrested immediately, sent to a concentration camp and were never heard from again.

For the most part, my schoolmates didn't pay much attention to the yellow badge. A few hurled insults at me as I passed, but I was used to being called a *sale Juif,* a 'dirty Jew,' and I learned to keep my temper. I knew it was imperative that I be immune to such provocations and maintain a low profile; but sometimes it was extremely difficult.

Eventually, we got used to wearing the yellow star in public, though we removed it whenever we could do so without being caught. As we passed others wearing the star on the street, we quickly exchanged glances and continued on in silence. It became extremely difficult to hide or pretend we were like everybody else. At school, only a handful of students wore the star because most of the Jews in the neighborhood had either been arrested or had gone into hiding.

After the war, we learned that the yellow star, as well as all the other degrading and isolating schemes of the government, the arrests and the deportations, were all ideas conceived and authorized by the Nazi military commanders, Heinrich Himmler and Adolf Eichmann, who had been named the chief administrator of *die*

Endlösung der Judenfrage, 'the Final Solution of the Jewish Question.'

It was not the first time in Jewish history that Jews had been so intentionally degraded and compelled to wear distinctive clothing and emblems. In the Middle Ages, similar practices had been devised in various Christian countries, in Spain and Germany. But we were living in the modern era, in a period following the so-called 'Enlightenment.' How could this happen? What was it that allowed for such a cultural regression? I remembered what Monsieur Spector had taught us in Hebrew School, and I thought—*If Jesus of Nazareth was among us today, he too would have to wear a yellow star.*

During the summer months, the arrests intensified. Twelve members of my own family were arrested and deported. My cousin, Rafael, returned home from work one day to find a notice on the door of his house ordering him to present himself at the police station immediately. His wife, Haika, had been arrested in the morning, only an hour after he had left for work. He stopped at our house on his way to the police station to say goodbye. He looked pale and nervous and spoke haltingly. When my grandmother suggested that he go into hiding, he said that he wanted to be with his wife, "to protect her." Placing his gold watch on the table, he said, "If I ever come back, you can return it to me; but if I don't, give it to one of the children."

That was the last time we ever saw him.

A few weeks later, we received a postcard from our cousin, Haika. It had been written in the Baune la Rolande camp, some forty miles south of Paris, but the postmark indicated that it had been mailed from a little town in the Eastern part of France, almost on the border with Germany. It had probably been thrown from one of the cattle-cars traveling in the direction of Germany. A passer-by must have found it near the railroad tracks, and seeing that its stamp had not been canceled, put it in a mailbox.

The hurriedly written letter read:

Dear Aunt,

I just left Beaune la Rolande for an unknown destination. At this very moment, I am on the train. I heard that we may be traveling toward Metz, after that [. . .] Dear Anna, I hope you will write to me when I can give you a fixed address. Let me know if my husband is in Paris or if he has been caught [by the police].

I would appreciate your sending me at once a parcel with my overcoat, some skirts and dresses and some sugar, as I left in a ridiculous hurry.

I thank you in advance and I send you my love. Please let me know if my husband has received my card. I will work for the Germans [. . .] I will write to you once I am liberated.

Mme. Haya Slovo
Beaune la Rolande,
Baraque 19.

Our cousin Haika was letting us know that she was being "relocated" to a labor camp, somewhere in the East. She seemed to have no idea that this 'relocation' meant that she would never come back from this journey. The names Rafael and Haika Slovo Dembitzer appear on the lists of victims at the Memorial de la Shoah in Paris.

Chère tante —

Je suis partie de Beaune la Rolande pour destination inconnue. En ce moment je voyage en train. il paraît que nous allons à Metz puis après.... Chère Anna je te prie de m'écrire quand tu connaîtras mon adresse fixe. Si mon mari est à Paris s'il est pris. je te prierai de m'envoyer un colis car je suis partie comme une folle. J'ai un besoin urgent de man teau, jupes, foulards, robes, sucre, si tu peux du pain azyme.

Je te remercie d'avance
et je t'embrasse bien
fort.
Écris-moi si mon mari
a reçu ma carte. Car
il pourrait m'envoyer
un certificat, parce que
il travaille pour
les Allemands et
je serai libérée,
enfin peut être!
j'arrête.
Voici mon adresse
d'avant (ils vont art
suivre)
Mme Sharco Haya.
à Beaune-la-Rolande
Baraque 19
(Loiret)

My cousin Haika's letter, probably thrown from the train near Metz.

The French politicians learned well from the Germans and quickly blamed all the food shortages and rationing we had to endure on "the traitors and the enemies of freedom"—Jews, Gypsies, Communists and homosexuals. And to this group, they now added the British. The British 'aggressors' were now made equally responsible for the evils of war, and newscasters on the radio ended their program with the words—borrowed from one of Napoleon's generals—*Et l'Angleterre comme Carthage sera détruite*, 'England, like Carthage, will be destroyed!'

Of course, we put no faith in the information broadcast by the National French Radio, as it was obviously manipulated by the German Ministry of Propaganda. The radio and newspapers of France had become mere tools with which the Germans could manipulate public opinion. The only reliable source of information we had came from the British Broadcasting Corporation's news program in French.

Though the Germans had forbidden us to listen to any foreign radio stations, they couldn't block signal and thus our neighbors listened to the Voice of Free France on the BBC—*Les Français parlent aux Français*, "The French are speaking to the French"—every night. We often joined them in the courtyard of our cluster of houses to hear the news, to which we listened with an almost religious solemnity. That is how we learned the Germans were facing great resistance from the Russian army and was beginning to retreat from some areas it had previously held. We also learned that the United States had declared war on Japan after an unprovoked attack on Pearl Harbor, and that the Allies were now advancing in North Africa and were on their way to liberate Europe.

These broadcasts were also mysterious and

intriguing, because they were always preceded by a number of coded messages meant for the Maquisards, the freedom fighters of the French Underground. They used phrases like, "The crows returned to their nest" or "The bear is dancing in the woods." Naturally, I was fascinated by these cryptic messages and wondered how many people understood what they meant and what specific instructions they contained. To us, they mostly signified hope; they told us that someone was fighting for us, and that the smaller forces of the Underground were in communication with the much larger forces of the Allies.

From time to time, the BBC rebroadcast portions of the historic address of General Charles de Gaulle, the head of the French Free Forces, when he announced the capitulation of France in 1940, and during which he had declared—*La France a perdu une bataille, mais la France n'a pas perdu la guerre!*—"France has lost a battle, but France has not lost the war!"

This motto had become a source of pride and hope for all of us; but the French battalion was too small to be victorious on its own. With the Soviet army engaged elsewhere, it was only when America declared war on Japan and Germany that a defeat of the Nazi war machine became a real possibility to us.

Some of my classmates also listened to these broadcasts, and together we followed the advances of the Allies on a big map of Europe which rolled-up above the blackboard. Of course, we pretended to be looking at some region in France for geography when we were actually looking at Stalingrad or the Ukraine. Our teachers were always careful not to discuss the war so as not to contradict the official accounts given us by the authorities.

One morning, we witnessed a strange and frightening incident during the break. As we were all in the courtyard, two policemen entered and proceeded to the secretariat. I was afraid they had come to arrest students wearing the yellow star. I quickly debated whether I should take off the sweater on which my yellow star had been sewn or simply go and hide in the bathroom. But, before I had even decided on a course of action, they came out of the office, only a minute or so later, and went straight to the teachers' meeting room. Apparently, they wanted to 'talk' to Monsieur R., the mathematics teacher for the ninth and tenth graders.

The other teachers said that he had been in the meeting room only a few minutes before, but they did not know where he had gone. The policemen then went to his classroom and waited near the door, ready to talk to him the moment he arrived. But he never came back!

We later learned that the police had come to arrest Monsieur R., having received information from a collaborator that indicated he was working under a false name. They also had reason to believe that he was a Jew who had refused to register as such at the onset of the occupation. Thus, according to the regulations set up by the Commission for Jewish Affairs, he was teaching illegally.

What the police didn't know is that as soon as one of the secretaries overheard the name of the teacher the police had come to arrest, she quickly went into the next room and called Monsieur R. on the telephone to warn him that the police were looking for him. He then left the college in great haste through an emergency exit and that is why they couldn't find him!

When I told my mother about the teacher, she said that this was the reason she had hesitated to purchase a false identity card from the members of the Underground; she was afraid that the police might discover the fraud and arrest them all. But in this case, it was not the fault of his documents, but the malevolent denunciation of one person determined to harm another. These kinds of things happened over and over again during the German Occupation of France: oppressors and collaborators worked together to hunt down the persecuted, while kind and courageous people sought to protect and help them. In the midst of the war between the Axis powers and the Allies, there was another kind of war going on in the occupied territories.

In the weeks that followed, my mother, fearing that she might be arrested for not obeying the regulations, gave up her part-time job in the dress shop.

A few weeks later, she saw a want-ad in the monthly bulletin of the UGIF (Union Générale des Israélites de France) looking for a social worker for the Rothschild Orphanage of the Rue Lamblardie in Paris. She applied and was hired almost immediately.

Her task consisted of taking care of some twenty elderly people who were hiding in the orphanage. The administrators of the orphanage clearly hoped that the police would not dare arrest these people on humanitarian grounds. The police must have known that there were elderly people living in the orphanage, but thus far had shown no interest in them.

On several occasions, I visited my mother at the orphanage and got acquainted with the residents who were volunteering in the office. They were amazing people! One of them was Colonel Weill, who was in his early seventies. He had served in the French army after being drafted at the onset of World War I and retired much later with the rank of colonel. There was also Jean B., who was only in his forties, but who was completely blind. He was a talented pianist and would regale us with concerts at the end of the day. The executive secretary, Ruth G., had been a distinguished professor

93

of French literature until the authorities had forbidden her to teach. The director of the orphanage, Monsieur Cohen, lived in the home with his family. His son, who was older than I, taught me how to play basketball in the courtyard adjacent to the main building.

My mother worked at the orphanage for a few months, until warned by our neighbor, Madame Paquet, that the police were planning a raid on the institution. She resigned her post immediately. Two days later, the police arrested a number of the residents of the home. There was no compassion whatsoever; the police simply executed the order as they had been instructed.

The residents of the nearby Rothschild Home for the Aged were also arrested at that time and sent to concentration camps. Many of them could not even walk without assistance, but were still taken away to be "relocated in the East," as it said in the official reports.

These seemingly surgical arrests and deportations were simply a part of the graduated plan of the Nazi's "final solution to the Jewish problem," approved by Hitler and his associates at the Wannsee Conference in January of 1942. Looking back, it is hard to believe that the French authorities did not know the fate of those who were deported. They certainly knew that many would die in the sealed cattle cars taking them to the camps. They also knew that the Jews who were relocated in the East would never return; for as soon as they were arrested, their apartments were emptied and their businesses liquidated. Thus, the French government was a willing accomplice in the German plan to annihilate the Jewish people.

I remember a tragic episode that happened in the suburb of Neuilly. The Germans had suspected a man of having a connection with the Underground and decided to arrest him. When they knocked at the door of his apartment, the man saw two uniformed German policemen through the peephole. He then picked up his revolver, opened the door, and before they had time to react, shot both men! After the German High Command learned that the man was Jewish, they rounded up a hundred Jews in Neuilly and sent them directly to the concentration camp at Drancy. This was a warning to other Jews who might consider resisting the orders of the German police.

Nevertheless, the Germans were unable to crush the patriotic zeal of the French people, and many young men joined the Underground in spite of the dangers. Their units usually concentrated their actions in the more remote areas of the countryside, hoping to spare the local population from German reprisals.

In one instance, a German convoy was ambushed by the French Free Forces on the road leading to the town of Oradour-sur-Glane, near Limoges. The Germans suffered a number of casualties, and in retaliation, gathered several hundred inhabitants of the town in a church, locked the doors, and set the building on fire. Only a few escaped the flames. The massacre at Oradour-sur-Glane was one of the most gruesome episodes of the German occupation of France.

But there were many such confrontations between the Germans and the Underground. Once, my cousin Gabriel told me that the truck in which he and half a dozen of his comrades were hidden under bales of hay was stopped by the Germans at a roadblock. They searched the truck and eventually found the young men. In the ensuing gun battle, the German soldiers killed or wounded every member of the French resistance except him as he had managed to hide under the truck. The Germans, who had also suffered several casualties, abandoned the truck on the side of the road and left the dead and wounded scattered on the ground. My cousin then ran to a nearby farm and asked for assistance to care for the wounded. He was later decorated with a medal of valor for the help he had brought to his comrades. The Maquisards were ready to give their lives for their country.

I often wished I were older so I could fight the Nazis in the Underground, but I was only a schoolboy. Still, I wanted to stand up for the cause.

Once, as I was walking to the subway after school with some of my classmates, they started a discussion about the Jews. One of them said that Jews were all cowards and cheats, and that you could never trust a Jew because they would always end up betraying you, just as they had betrayed Jesus.

Well, I couldn't help replying to this ridiculous assault, so I said: "That's not true; Jews are just like everybody else, and most of them are honest people!"

"Liar!" he said. "You, dirty Jew—my uncle knows better than you!"

"People are sometimes mistaken," I replied.

"I'll show you what you deserve!" he said, and he punched me in the face. I tried to fight back, but he was too strong for me. He punched me again and blood began to run down my face. At that point, the others intervened and held him back.

I went back to the school and asked to see the nurse. The secretary in the office told me that she had just left for the day, but seeing the blood gushing over my face, quickly found the proper key and took me to the infirmary herself. She cleaned the wound with a red solution and put a bandage over the bruise on my face. She then asked me how this had happened, and I told her that I had been attacked by a classmate who claimed all Jews were cowards and cheats.

She asked for the boy's name, but I said: "Madame, I'd rather just forget about it. If I complain, it will probably just aggravate the situation. I'll be more careful in the future."

"Alright," she said, "but if it happens again, I'll have to report it to the dean."

I thanked her for her discretion, and for taking care of my wound, and was prepared to leave, when she said: "The Nazis and their friends have poisoned the minds of so many people that even children cannot have a civil conversation without spewing some hatred; it's very sad."

I never told anyone the name of the boy who had attacked me, but the secretary asked around discretely and found out who he was. She called his mother to let her know what her son had done, and the woman apologized profusely. She explained that her brother-in-law was a member of the militia, and each time he came for a visit, he lashed-out against the Jews and Communists. In this way, he had probably influenced her son with his tirades. She said she would do her best to correct the situation without saying a word about the incident. I don't know what his mother said to him, or what she did to correct the situation, but he never said a word to me again after the incident.

VIII
Going into Hiding

AS THE ARRESTS INCREASED in Paris and its surrounding areas, my mother decided that the time had finally come for us to go into hiding. She asked my brother and me to listen carefully as she spoke to us one evening:

"Children," she said, "the situation is getting worse, and it is becoming very dangerous for us in the city. Whole families are being arrested and deported every day for no reason. We can't wait any longer; we have to make a decision right now. I think it will be best for both of you to spend some time in the country with a family of farmers. You may not know them, but it will only be for a short time, maybe a year, until the war comes to an end.

"Early tomorrow morning, we're leaving for Evron. I've already spoken to a couple of farmers and they will take care of you. I hope they will treat you well. I don't want to do this, but if we don't act quickly, I'm afraid we may all be arrested and sent to concentration camps. I'll prepare a little suitcase with some of your clothes for each of you, and you will take it with you to the farm."

"But, Mother," I said, "why can't you come with us?"

"You know that Grandma is not in very good health and cannot travel easily; I must stay here to take care of her."

Both my brother and I shook our heads and said: "We understand; if this is what we have to do, we'll do it and try do be good."

"Remember, children, *you must not let any one know you are Jewish,* under any circumstance. You both have baptismal certificates with the name 'Leon,' and from now on, you must behave like other Catholic boys in the region, until France is liberated."

Then, with tears in her eyes, she said, "Even if grandmother and I are arrested and deported, I want you to survive the war . . ."

Mother didn't waste any time. She carefully removed the yellow stars from our clothes and prepared little suitcases for each of us.

The next morning, at dawn, we all went to the Gare Montparnasse. The policemen standing at the entrance to the railroad station let us go without asking to see our papers. Mother bought three tickets, and we took the first express train to Le Mans. We then waited a half an hour for an omnibus train that would take us to Evron.

Once in Evron, we waited again for the bus to Sainte Gemmes le Robert, from which we walked slowly to the farm of Monsieur Etienne and Madame Bardou. After a short conversation, they agreed to take me in as a paying guest. Mother told them she wanted to make sure that I would have enough nourishment to stay in good health, and also let them know that she would not be able to come to Normandy as often in the coming months.

Madame Bardou took us out to the stable where I was installed in a corner of an enclosure on a small mattress of straw in a wooden box. Madame Bardou gave me a blanket to keep me warm and a little towel with which to dry myself after washing. I then embraced my mother and brother and said, "*Au revoir, Maman et Robert.*" Then I assured my mother, "I'll be good, Mama."

She replied, "May God be with you and your new family!"

They took leave of me, and Lucien Bardou took my mother and brother to the farm of a nearby family my mother had befriended on previous visits. Like the Bardous, they had agreed to take my brother in as a paying guest also.

I walked around the buildings of the farm for a while, exploring my new surroundings, and then had a light supper with the Bardous. They asked me my age and what I was studying in Paris, and then told me that the next day they would show me some of the things I could do on the farm or out in the fields. After this, I said goodnight and went to my bed in the stable.

I was alone in the stable with the horses. When the little candle Madame Bardou had given me went out, I lay down on my makeshift bed and waited for the horses to lie down. I didn't know then that, unlike humans, horses could sleep standing up. So I fell asleep in my bed while waiting.

Eventually, I got used to living in the stable and the smell of manure, and I quickly came to appreciate the company of the horses.

On the farm, there was no running water, no sewage system, no electricity or telephone. Nevertheless, the Bardous managed to live pretty well without these amenities. Everyone always had a task to perform: the farmer and his sons were working in the fields almost every day, and his wife and daughters were always busy doing various chores around the farm — milking the cows, feeding the animals, and taking care of the vegetable garden.

101

On most days, I would accompany the farmer and his sons and do whatever they asked me to do. I built a wall with rocks scattered in the fields and gathered dry wood for the fire. On other days, I stayed around the farm and helped the farmer's wife with her chores.

Sunday was a special day at the farm. We didn't go to the fields on Sundays (except during the harvest time), and Madame Bardou always prepared an elaborate *déjeuner* or lunch before we went to church. Often this was a *lapin au cidre*, a rabbit stew cooked in fermented apple cider. My job consisted of selecting two rabbits from their cage (preferably fat ones) and bringing them to the farmer. He would then bind their hind legs with a string and hang them from the top of the open door of the barn. Then, taking a pair of sharp scissors, he pierced the eyes of the rabbits (killing them instantly, as the scissors went into the brain) and let the blood drain from them. He then flayed them so that I could bring them to Madame Bardou, who cut them up and put them in a big cauldron with an assortment of vegetables and spices. She would then pour a big pitcher of cider on top of the stew and would let it cook slowly in the fireplace until we came back from town.[*]

When everything was prepared for the *déjeuner*, we would get up on the horse-drawn carriage and go to Evron, some six miles away. The farmer and his two sons would then go to the Café de l'Eglise, where they would meet with other farmers from the area and talk about local events and what was going on in the world over a bottle of *Calvados*, an apple brandy or fermented cider. At the same time, I went to church with the farmer's wife and her two daughters. In this way, I learned to follow the Mass in Latin and to sing most of

---

[*] At other times, a chicken fricassee was on the Sunday menu; and on Christmas and other festive occasions, we might have a roast goose as a special treat.

the hymns with the choir.

When the Mass was over, we would go to the café to meet the farmer and his sons, and then return to the farm to partake of the *déjeuner* which was waiting for us in the cauldron hanging in the fireplace.

In the afternoon, I would feed the ducks or the rabbits or pick flowers in the fields. When the farmer's youngest daughter was not with one of her friends, I often played cards or dominos with her.

For an entire year, I didn't attend school or read even a single book, except for a few pages of the missal in church on Sunday mornings. Deciphering the Latin of the Catholic Mass was a challenge, but I did my best and was often able to recognize the root of most of the words that had evolved into modern French. Within a few months, I had become reasonably familiar with the themes of the liturgy and was able to chant quietly with the priest.

One Sunday, after the Mass, the priest asked me to come and see him in the rectory. I told Madame Bardou and promised to meet the family at the café as soon as my meeting with the priest was done.

"Michel," the priest said, "you're not from this area, are you?"

"No, Father, I'm from Bagnolet, a suburb of Paris; but," I added, as my mother had instructed me to, "I was born in Laval."

"Did you attend catechism classes in Bagnolet?"*

"No, Father; the church was too far from our home and my mother could not take me to the classes because

---

* Basic instruction in Catholic doctrines.

103

she worked in the city."

"Did you ever study the principles of our faith? Did your parents teach you these?"

"Father," I said, "we were not very observant, and like most people in Bagnolet, we didn't go to church very often. I don't know much, but I am catching up. I can now follow the Mass, and I think I understand nearly half of it."

"That's fine, my son," the priest said, "but you are not yet attending the catechism classes in our church, and I think the time has come for you to take your first Communion.* How would you like to join the class so you can participate in the celebration which will take place in just a few months?"

"Father," I said, "I would like to, but my whole family lives near Paris, and I would prefer to celebrate my first Communion with them. Can I postpone it?"

"Yes, my son, I understand. These are difficult times and we must make concessions. That's fine. We will be patient and wait another year. Hopefully, by that time, the war will be over."

Relieved, I took my leave of the priest.

I had assumed this identity without much difficulty and had conducted myself in the way my mother had instructed me to do. But I wasn't sure whether the priest had really accepted my reasons as genuine, or whether he suspected that I was only pretending to be Catholic. In truth, I was tempted to say "Yes" to him, for I would have liked to join the other boys and girls in the celebration; but something prevented me from acquiescing to his request, something deep within me.

---

* The Eucharist, or symbolic partaking of the body (bread) and blood (wine) of Jesus Christ.

I walked to the café and waited until the farmer had offered his final round of drinks and then we all went back to the farm for our Sunday lunch.

During our evening meals, I could sometimes pick-up a few scraps of information about the war: a few scattered details about the activities of the Underground in our area, the progress made by the Russians and the Americans on their respective fronts, and the heavy losses being sustained by the German army.

But the Bardous were less interested in the war than they were in their farm. They seemed to have no time for reading books or newspapers or listening to the radio. Indeed, they didn't even own a radio receiver. Everything they knew about what was happening in the world they learned on Sunday mornings in the café from its manager who summarized the news for them.

Like the rest of the farmers, they were most interested in the fluctuations of the price of wheat or milk or cattle, though they could not ignore what was happening in the rest of the world altogether. Nevertheless, as they saw it, they were doing what they did best, working hard to produce food for the inhabitants of the region and, for the most part, trusted their political leaders to defend the interests of the nation.

From time-to-time, they visited other farm families and attended weddings and funerals, but apart from Sunday mornings spent at Mass and in the café, this was all the social life they had.

Every three or four months, the Bardous would slaughter a pig and make a kind of stew-paté, known as *rillettes* in Normandy. They cut the meat in small pieces and added some salt and spices, cooking the mixture in a big cauldron for many hours before filling a number of earthenware terrines with the stew. They then let these cool until the fat had formed a protective layer over the surface, after which, they covered the terrines with brown paper and placed them in the cool of the pantry.

Through the year, our diet consisted mainly of *rillettes*-spread on a slice of country bread with a bowl of soup, except of course, on weekends and holidays.

The farm itself was situated at the end of a dirt path, which was not easily accessible from the main road. Nevertheless, this did not discourage occasional visits from German soldiers who came to the farm on their motorcycles. They usually argued with the Bardous, pressuring them for some extra bacon and eggs, even though this was against regulations. The farmers were already required to bring their excess products to a collection center, where the French authorities, acting on behalf of the Germans, took a portion of them for the Germans and distributed the rest to the local and national markets.

Whenever I saw a German soldier approaching the farm, I walked swiftly back to the stable and stayed there until he left. He probably would not have recognized me as a Jew, but I was afraid he might ask me a question which would somehow lead him to suspect that I was a Jew in hiding. I had no desire to tempt fate in this way, to endanger myself or the Bardous.

One Sunday, we learned that the Underground operating in the vicinity of Evron had successfully raided the German armory, taking away weapons and ammunition to use in their own acts of sabotage. On another occasion, the Maquisards attacked a German convoy that was transporting military supplies and blew up a truck, inflicting heavy losses on the enemy. A few Germans were killed and others wounded. In the aftermath of these attacks, the Germans resolved to concentrate their forces in one military outpost near the city. Undeterred, the resistance fighters strengthened their numbers in the same area.

One Sunday afternoon, Jacqueline, a niece of Monsieur Bardou, surprised us all with a visit. She brought a *tarte aux pommes* made with sliced apples, saying that she wanted to celebrate a happy event with her uncle and aunt and her cousins. As we were all gathered around the table, she told us an amazing story:

"I want to tell you what happened to me last week. It's confidential of course, but you are my family, and I know you aren't going to jeopardize my well-being by reporting me to my boss. Just listen to my story and you'll be proud of me.

"You know that I work for the police department in Evron. Well, last Tuesday morning, I was asked to take a report to the head officer of the German *polizei* on the outskirts of town. So I placed the report in my purse and rode my bicycle out to their headquarters. The building was heavily guarded and the German soldiers asked me the purpose of my visit. I told them I had been sent by my superior to deliver some documents to the Commandant. They checked my identity card and my purse, and took me to the Commandant's office and told me to wait for a moment.

"While I was alone in the office, I saw a number of papers on the desk and I was suddenly tempted to look at them. At first, I hesitated to do so, but a moment later, almost without even realizing it, I found myself standing next to the desk and glancing at one of the papers. It must have been only a few seconds, because I was back in my seat the moment the Commandant entered his office to greet me and I delivered the report to him. He glanced at it and said that it was fine and that

I could leave.

"A German guard accompanied me to the gate. I took my bicycle and rode back to the city. Instead of returning to the police station, however, I went to the Café de l'Eglise and asked the owner to call my friend Pierre. I waited a few minutes for Pierre to arrive and then we entered the billiard room and sat down in the dark.

"'Pierre' I said, 'I just delivered a report to the Commandant of the *polizei*. While I was waiting in his office, I managed to peek at the papers lying on his desk. All I remember is an address. They may have that house under surveillance. So please let our friends know at once that the house at 22 Rue du Marché is not safe anymore; the Germans are probably watching it.'

"Pierre thanked me and assured me that he would inform his friends without delay."

We were all spellbound by Jacqueline's account. We asked her if she knew what happened after she informed Monsieur Pierre, and he said:

"You won't believe it. The leaders of the Underground had planned a meeting in that house on that very evening! If they had not been warned, they would all have been arrested and likely tortured to reveal their plans and their hiding places. I was so happy that I was able to help them and prevent a catastrophe that I wanted to celebrate with all of you!"

In the weeks that followed, Jacqueline continued to inform Pierre whenever she thought the Underground might benefit from some information that was passing her desk. She asked us never to mention her name or any of the details of her story. Thus, Jacqueline became one of the quiet heroes of the Underground.

IX
A German Raid

ONE EVENING, as we were about to sit down for dinner, a well-dressed young man in his twenties came running up to the farm. Monsieur Bardou invited him to sit down and rest so that he might catch his breath. He was breathing heavily and clearly exhausted. After a few minutes, he had begun to recover and said:

"My name is Paul L. from L'Ermitage and I would like to ask your permission to stay the night. I could sleep in the barn or the stable. But I must tell you, the Germans are looking for me. They think I was involved in last week's raid on the convoy in which two German soldiers were killed."

Monsieur Bardou listened attentively and said, "You may stay at the farm for the night . . . And let's hope that none of us will get into trouble."

Then Monsieur Bardou asked the young man to go for a walk with him and I went out to my bed in the stable. I undressed and I lay down on my straw bed. I recited Psalm 91, which I knew by heart, and said a special prayer for the welfare of the young man who was trying to escape from the German police.

The next morning, I was awakened early by the barking of the dogs and the noise of a patrol car pulling into the courtyard of the farm. I jumped up and peeked through the windows. I could see three German soldiers getting out of a military car and walking toward the house. In very poor French, one of them informed

Monsieur Bardou that they were looking for a fugitive and that they had orders to search every building in the area.

As he said this, another soldier stood in the courtyard while two others began their search. Without waiting for an invitation, they entered the house and looked in every room with their flashlights. They ordered the girls to get out of their beds so that they might make sure no one was hiding under them. They searched every corner of the house and then went out to the barn where they moved a number of bales of hay and straw to make sure that no one was hiding behind them.

Having completed their search of the barn, they proceeded to the cow stable and finally to the horse stable. I was just getting dressed when they suddenly appeared in front of me. The German who spoke some French asked me if someone had been hiding in the stable, and I answered that I was the only one in the stable. They looked between the stalls and under a bale of hay and then turned to me again and asked if I had seen a stranger on the farm the night before. I answered that I had not seen anyone besides my family.

They left the stable and continued their search in the other outbuildings. They looked in the shed where the ploughs and the other equipment were stored and pointed their flashlights at the carriage and the wagon. Then they checked the chicken coop and even the space behind the rabbits' cage, but found nothing.

Without a word, they went back to their car and left the farm. As we were still recovering from the shock, we suddenly saw the young man appear in the courtyard of the farm. Monsieur Bardou invited him in to have breakfast with us and said:

"We've had quite a scare, Paul. We'd all have been

arrested if they'd found you on the farm. I'm grateful to God that you were not, but I'm curious . . . *Where were you hiding?*"

"I'll tell you, Monsieur Bardou. After we said 'good night' last evening, I looked for the perfect place to hide on your farm. I knew the Germans would concentrate their search on the buildings that offered the best hiding places, like the barn and stable, and for that very reason, I avoided them. After thinking about it for a while, I decided to hide under the back bench of the carriage, wrapped up in the blanket I found there. The Germans pointed their flashlights at the carriage, and must have seen the blanket under the seat, but clearly didn't suspect that anyone was hiding in it!

"I am most grateful to you, Monsieur and Madame Bardou, for saving my life. I am also proud of you because you kept your calm and did not get in a panic when the Germans interrogated you and searched the farm. Even the boy who sleeps in the stable knew what to say to the Germans. Again, thank you all!"

Had the Germans found him, we would all have been arrested. If he had resisted, they would likely have killed him and accused us of assisting a fugitive.

"What are you going to do now?" asked Monsieur Bardou.

Confidently, the young man said: "I'll wait for the milkman to come and collect the milk. Then I'll get on his truck and hide between the milk containers and go with him back to town where I can stay at any of our safe houses."

"And what is your plan after that?" asked Monsieur Bardou.

"That," he said, "will depend upon the orders I receive from my commander."

We said, *Au revoir et bonne chance!* 'Good-bye and good luck!' to the young man who went to the stable to wait for the milkman.

For myself, I was proud of having found the courage to speak with confidence to the Germans. I knew I had contributed, albeit in a minor way, to preventing a catastrophe for the family. And I was thrilled at having personally witnessed this young man's bravery. It helped me realize that Jews were not the *only* targets of the Nazis.

The next Sunday at the café in Evron, Monsieur Bardou told his friends in a low voice about the exploits of young Paul L.. They were all impressed and admired the young man for the way he had managed to elude the Germans. I never saw the young man again, but I have no doubt that he returned to his unit in the Maquis and he went on fighting for the cause.

X
Winter on the Farm

ONCE AUTUMN ARRIVED, the temperature began to drop steadily and I began to feel the cold at night. The farmer and his children, whose bedrooms were in the house, had a fireplace to keep them warm; but the only source of heat in the stable was the warmth of the horses' bodies and their exhalation. On the really cold nights, I slept in my clothes and overcoat.

The horses played an important role in the farmer's operations. Since there was no tractor on the farm, he relied on 'horse power' for everything from sowing to harvesting, for transporting the crops, the hay and the straw, the wood and the apples from the orchard, and also for going to town on Sundays or holidays. During the winter months, when there was little need for them, they were still taken into a field near the farmhouse for most of the day. After a snowfall or during a storm, they would stay in their stable.

The youngest horse was six months old and I thought of him as my pet. I had named him Champion (because I wanted him to win competitions one day). He was brown and just about my height. He loved having his neck caressed and often ate the carrots I would bring him right from my hand. I talked to him whenever I got a chance, and when he shook his head, I took this as a sign that he agreed with me. When he was not with the mare who had foaled him, we would play together outside. I often ran after him in the field and, on occasion, he would even follow me.

When it was raining or snowing outside, I would spend most of the day in the family room, helping Madame Bardou peel potatoes or onions, or breaking dry branches to throw in the fireplace. The farmer and his sons usually played cards and I would watch them. The children were much older than I, and I often felt like a baby among them. On occasion, I would have a short conversation with one of them and they were always amused by my way of speaking. They would say something like:

"You talk just like those Parisians who come here during the summer months! The moment you see them, you know they aren't farmers. They speak with that light, singing voice, as if they were ready to give a recital. Not the kind of people who know how to plough a field or harvest a crop of wheat. Their hands are too soft for the work we do in the country."

"Just give me time and I'll get there." I would say.

The farmer's sons were 16 and 18 years old, respectively. They were tall young men and well built. They had no need to work out in a gym; they got their exercise on the farm. But the daughters were more delicate; they liked to sew or knit when they didn't have another task to perform. My mother brought them skeins of wool or cotton whenever she came to visit us.

In no time at all, I got used to living on the farm.

I soon came to realize that the farmer and his family were running a complex enterprise that was far more demanding than I had ever imagined. Every member of the family was on duty almost all the time. I got acquainted with many of the tasks that had to be performed on a regular basis and tried to help whenever I could. Although I had no experience, I was eager to learn how to be a farmer. I would carefully observe them as they were doing their chores so that I might take my turn the moment I was able to do so. Before long, I asked if I could feed the horses and was occasionally allowed to do this.

When I asked Monsieur Bardou if I could learn to ride a horse, he told me that my mother had asked him not to let me ride as she was afraid I might fall and injure myself. Nevertheless, he promised to teach me how to drive the mare that pulled the carriage when we went to town, and I looked forward to holding the reins like an adult. Later, I found that this really didn't take much effort, as she knew her way back and forth and simply trotted at her usual pace.

When Christmas came, we all dressed up and went to church in the evening. The church was decorated with banners and the nave was full to capacity. I felt comforted by the idea that all these good people were actually celebrating the birth of a Jewish child who had become the central figure in the Christian faith. "This amazing fact," my Hebrew School teacher in Paris had said, "is the most remarkable proof that the Jews never constituted an inferior race."

As I listened to the story of the Nativity, I thought, *Just as the Judeans were persecuted in the days of Jesus, the Jews are being persecuted today. It is as if nothing has changed in almost two thousand years!* Then I wondered whether there was another hidden Jewish boy or girl here among the Christian worshippers.

At the end of the Mass, the priest shook hands with everyone that had come, often saying "It's so nice to see you here tonight." I wondered if he was thinking to himself—*I see you so seldom the rest of the year!* But he was cheerful and cordial with everyone. I said, "Merry Christmas, Father," and he responded with a smile. Once again, I wondered whether or not he knew I was

Jewish. But he was a compassionate man and did not seem to be concerned with these kinds of questions.

The next day, we had a number of visitors at the farm, and in the afternoon, we visited several other farms. I saw my brother and we smiled at each other; we wished each other a *"Joyeux Noel,"* and added, "In a few months, it will all be over." The farmers all took leave of one another, expressing the hope that this would be the last Christmas they would celebrate under the Germans. The Christmas wishes of 'peace and goodwill' were taken seriously by all the inhabitants of the country in those days.

When my mother came for a visit, she always brought presents for everyone at the farm, and everyone looked forward to seeing her. We would take a little walk around the farm and she would tell me about my grandmother, our extended family and our neighbors in Bagnolet. She would also tell me the news she had heard on the BBC. In turn, I would tell her what had happened on the farm and what we had learned at the café in Evron. Before we parted, she would reassure me that the war was nearing its end and that the Germans would soon be forced to retreat from France and leave us in peace: "We must be patient—another six months or a year—and we will go back to a normal life. We must pray for the liberation of Europe and the end of the Nazi regime. May God hear our prayers."

One of the young Bardous would then take my mother to the farm where my brother was living and she would return to Paris by the last train, hoping that she would not be asked to present her identity card until she was back in the city. She displayed an amazing sense of confidence whenever she passed a policeman, and always had a few words to make them laugh. Often, she passed numerous check-points without having to

116

present her papers by simply telling the policeman a funny story with a big smile. Sometimes, she would tell them that she had forgotten her identity card at her boyfriend's apartment. They would laugh and let her go.

Even though the Bardous were kind to me, I was always sad and overcome with loneliness when my mother returned to Paris. Deep in my heart, I knew I did not belong to their family. I was just a boarder that circumstances had brought to the farm. I had no friend my own age to play or chat with and, whenever I was with a group of children, I had to be extremely careful not to say anything that might reveal my true identity.

I enjoyed my life in the country, close to nature, but I also felt that I didn't really belong to the farming community. As a consequence, I often imagined myself in a different world. I yearned for the warmth and affection of my own family, for the embrace of my father, whom I had never known, and my mother who cared so deeply for me. I dreamt of becoming a pioneer in the land of my ancestors, a member of a *kibbutz* in Palestine, which I had once read about in a magazine. There, I would not be "a stranger in a strange land," but with my own people in the land of our ancestors.

But mostly I feared for my mother's safety when she left. I knew she had avoided arrest on many occasions, but I was always afraid she might not be as fortunate on her next trip. Moreover, the French police might decide to include French-born citizens in their next wave of arrests at any time.

Not wanting to betray my cover, I had decided not to take the little prayer book that had belonged to my mother with me to the farm. But I still recited the prayers I knew by heart, and even composed new ones every night before bed. I was confident that God would hear my prayers and protect my mother, my family and friends.

117

XI
Catherine's Wedding

FOR THE 20TH BIRTHDAY of the Bardou's eldest daughter, Catherine, a dinner was arranged at the Auberge de la Toque, the finest restaurant in Evron. Even though we were going through one of the most difficult periods of the war, the Bardous still felt that the coming-of-age of their daughter was an occasion to be celebrated in grand style. So, at the Bardou's request, the chef prepared some of the most exquisite dishes of the region, roast pheasant and braised venison, for which several hunters in the area donated their catch.

The sumptuous dinner was followed by a dance at which Catherine surprised everyone with her ease and gracefulness on the dance floor. All the young men waited their turn to dance with her, and she was able to renew her acquaintance with many old classmates whom she had not seen since she left middle school. As the evening came to an end, she thanked her parents and told them that this had been the most wonderful day of her life.

In the weeks that followed, Catherine was often invited out by her friends and their families on the weekend, until one Sunday, a few months after her birthday, a young man named Gérard came to the farm to have lunch with us. He came back a few times after that, until one day he arrived accompanied by his parents, Monsieur and Madame Desbois, who were farmers near Sainte Suzanne, a few miles away. The two families had a lively and jovial conversation for several hours and I soon understood that the Desbois had come to visit the Bardous in order to ask for the hand of Catherine for their son, Gérard.

The marriage was announced a few days later. It was to be held three weeks after Easter.

On the appointed day, we all went to City Hall for the civil ceremony, which was presided over by the mayor, and then to the Basilique Notre Dame de l'Epine for the religious ceremony, which was conducted by Father Marcel.

After the ceremonies were over, we all went to the Chalopiniére where the Bardous had arranged a banquet in honor of the newlyweds. Exquisite entrees were prepared by the chef of the Auberge de la Toque and some of his associates, and were all delivered by automobile to the farm a few hours before the banquet. An enormous wedding cake and confectioneries from the best baker in the area were also delivered, as well as a few cases of Calvados brandy and Champagne. Tables and chairs had been installed in the courtyard of the farm and beautiful tablecloths were spread over all the tables. A whole crew of servers in uniform had been hired for the occasion, and the hosts were ready to welcome the newlyweds and all their guests.

Even though the government had instituted a rigorous system of food rationing throughout the country, here in Normandy, people knew how to circumvent these restrictions. The farmers would simply not declare all the livestock they had, or all the wheat they harvested, and maintain a reserve of farm products for special occasions. In this way, we were able to forget the war for a few precious moments like this.

After the wedding cake was served, at the end of the

banquet, three musicians started to play and many people began to dance. At the same time, a dozen youngsters got up from their tables and went to a nearby field to run and to play. Four of us sat down in the field and started to play cards.

At one point, a boy named André said to me, "Michel, you cheated; you looked at my cards!"

"That's not true," I said, "Besides, you're holding them so close that *no one* could see them."

"You lie like a Jew," he retorted.

"I'm not lying! And what does lying have to do with Jews anyway?"

"All Jews are liars and cheats!"

I couldn't take it any more. I knew I had to tread carefully, but I couldn't let this comment pass.

"Have you ever met a Jew?" I challenged him.

"No," he answered.

"So how do you know they're all cheats?"

"I've heard people say it at school," he answered. Then he asked me, "Do you know any Jews?"

"Yes, and one was my friend in Paris until the police arrested him."

"You see! What did I tell you? All Jews are cheats, and *that's* why the police arrest them!"

"No, that's not the reason," I said, "because the police also arrested his little sister too, who was only three years old, and his grandmother, who was in a wheelchair."

"So why do they arrest Jews? There has to be a reason," he argued.

"I don't know," I said "but it's not because they're

cheats."

"I'm going to ask my dad," he said finally.

So we followed André between the tables until he found his father and asked him: "Dad, aren't all Jews cheaters? And isn't that why the police are arresting them?"

"No, André," said the father seriously, "they aren't. The Jews are arrested because Hitler doesn't like them. I know this for a fact, because there are Jewish families hiding in Evron and other towns in this area."

"What does a Jew look like? Do they have horns?" asked André.

"No, they don't . . . You can't tell a Jew from somebody else; they are just like us. If the police arrest them, it's because they have been ordered to by the Germans, just as they arrest members of the *Résistance*, or people who insult the Germans, saying *'sales Boches.'*"

This wonderful answer put an end of our dispute. We went back to the field and resumed our card game.

The party went on for another few hours. After sunset, everyone went home and I said goodnight to the Bardous.

The next morning, the farmer and his sons did not go out to the fields as usual; they had enough to do cleaning up after the activities of the day before. They had tables and chairs to fold, tablecloths and napkins to collect and pile. The rental company sent a small truck to collect all of these things, including the fine plates and silverware that they had rented for the party.

For the next three days, we ate leftovers from the banquet. Every member of the family had resumed their usual occupations except for Catherine and her husband, who went to St. Malo on their honeymoon to visit Mont Saint-Michel, one of the marvels of the world.

This was the first wedding I had ever attended and it made a strong impression on me. It gave me great satisfaction to have participated in a celebration of love and family at a time when so many were suffering under the German occupation and fearing for their lives. The only policeman present during the reception came to bring the greetings and congratulations of his colleagues to the newlywed couple. Even the milkman came to bring a card to the bride and groom. I was the only boy present who was not from the area and I appreciated the fact that I had been allowed to join the party. I was also glad that my disagreement with André over our game of cards did not cause a problem. He might easily have accused me of being a Jew, given my eagerness to defend them.

I yearned for the end of the war, for the restoration of my old life, for a time when I would not need to live in fear, always concealing my identity. I began to fantasize about how I would learn all about the history and the culture of my people and learn to practice openly the religion of my ancestors.

XII

A Visit to Mayenne

FOUR OR FIVE WEEKS after the wedding, the Bardous made plans to visit a widowed aunt of the farmer living in Mayenne, the administrative center of the district, some twenty five miles from the farm. His aunt Simone had been unable to attend Catherine's wedding because she was suffering from a severe cold. Thus, the Bardous decided to visit her in Mayenne after the wedding.

That day, we woke up earlier than usual and fed the animals while the women milked the cows. The milk cans were then placed in front of the stable for the milkman to collect. After these chores were completed, we all got up on the carriage and headed north on the D7, the departmental road which leads directly to Mayenne.

As we approached Aunt Simone's house, we were stopped by several policemen at a roadblock on the D7. They had orders to search every vehicle on the road for contraband, in particular, weapons or ammunition. They asked us to get out of the carriage so they might inspect it, but all they found were a few earthenware terrines filled with *rillettes* — a present for aunt Simone. Then they asked to see the identity cards of the adults and our destination. Monsieur Bardou answered that we were going to visit his aunt on the next street.

"What is your aunt's name?" asked one of the policemen.

"Madame Simone Jeannot," replied Etienne Bardou.

"I regret to inform you," said the policeman, "that Simone Jeannot was arrested just this morning and taken to the police station for questioning."

"What for?" he asked, alarmed.

"I don't know," said the policeman.

"In that case," he said, "we will go to the police station immediately. Can you tell us how to get there?"

He gave us directions and we went to the police station. I was to wait in the carriage, but as I needed to use the bathroom, I asked Monsieur Bardou if I could come with him into the station.

As soon as we were in the main office, he recognized the chief of police sitting at his desk. It just so happened they had done their military service in the same unit some twenty years before!

"Are you Raymond?" he asked the chief, "You must remember me; I'm Etienne Bardou. We served together some twenty years ago, in the 5th Squadron of the 12th Company after we were drafted. It's nice to see you again!"

"Yes, I remember you! Your parents owned a farm near Evron, right?"

"That's right" said Etienne, "and, if I remember well, your father drove the first automobile in Mayenne."

"That's right," said the chief, "and now I drive a patrol car here. But tell me, my friend, what brings you to Mayenne?"

"I came to visit my aunt Simone, but it looks like you are just as interested in her as I am. I can hear her talking in the other room. Why are you questioning her? She is a good person; she wouldn't harm a fly."

"Ah . . . Well it seems that she has some ties to the

Maquis, and my department head has requested that I find out more about her connections with them."

"What do you mean? Do you really suspect a 65-year-old woman of being involved with the *Résistance?* I can't believe it."

"I have to obey my orders," said the chief, "and so my assistant is questioning her. I've been asked to send a memo to the department head in Laval."

"Raymond, you are surely wasting your time; but it's not my business. It's almost lunchtime: how would you like some *rillettes* from the farm? The boy can go get them from the carriage."

Monsieur Bardou sent me out to the carriage and I retrieved one of the terrines of *rillettes*. He then offered them to the chief, who said: "That's good of you, Etienne. I appreciate the present. You know, it's become difficult to find good *rillettes* in Mayenne; the Germans like them so much that they buy up all our shipments!"

"We were planning to have them for lunch with my aunt; do you think she will be long?"

"It's just a formality," said the chief, "we were about to finish with her. You can take her home with you now."

The chief told his assistant that there was no need to pursue the interrogation any further and that she could go home with her nephew.

With a big smile, Etienne said, "Thank you, Raymond; I'll come to see you another time when you're not so busy and we can chat at leisure."

"Au revoir et merci pour les rillettes!" — Goodbye, and thanks for the paté! — said the chief with a wink that only a Norman countryman would have understood

fully.

Aunt Simone came out of a room adjacent to the office with an expression of relief.

"I'm so glad to see you!" she said. "Is your family with you?"

"Yes, Auntie Simone; they are all here except for Catherine and her husband, who are on their honeymoon at the Mont St. Michel."

"Then let's go home and have a nice lunch together."

Once we were in her house, she expressed her full gratitude to her nephew for his timely intervention.

"You could not have come and rescued me at a better time! I was getting tired of telling the inspector that I had never assisted any member of the *Résistance* in my life. It's is a lie, of course, but I could not endanger my friends."

"So you are involved with 'our friends,' Auntie Simone! I'm proud of you. I don't think the police will bother you again. The chief was a buddy of mine in the military and we forged a bond that is not easily broken. In any case, Auntie Simone, you must be more careful in the future."

"You don't have to tell me. From now on, I'll make it a rule that no one will come to my house during the day; they'll have to wait until dark, when no one can see who's knocking at my door!"*

"Have you allowed members of the *Résistance* to meet

---

* She had probably been denounced by a zealous collaborator who thought he was serving his country by cooperating with the authorities.

in your house!" asked Etienne, alarmed.

"Oh, no! I only provided temporary shelter to some young people who had nowhere else to go . . . And that's exactly what I told the policeman at the station."

After this, we had a lovely lunch in Aunt Simone's quaint little house and she told us some stories of the *Résistance* in Mayenne. She trusted her nephew implicitly and felt free to talk all about it to us.

When she had finished her stories, she turned to Etienne and asked, "Who is this boy who has come with you?"

"He's been staying with us for a few months," he said. "His mother lives in Paris and asked us to take him in because of the food shortages there. He's a daring little guy. When the Germans raided our farm a few weeks ago, they interrogated everyone and he understood the seriousness of the situation immediately and said nothing which might have endangered us."

"You know, Etienne, there are two children from Paris who have been placed with families in Mayenne, and we suspect they are Jewish children; but it doesn't make a difference: children are children, and we must take care of them."

Neither Aunt Simone nor the Bardous pursued the subject any further, but I'm sure they wondered whether I was Jewish as well.

Finally, we said goodbye and returned to La Chalopinière in time to milk the cows, feed the animals again and have a light supper.

The next day, the postman brought a postcard from the newlyweds mailed from St. Malo. Catherine described her visit to Mont St. Michel and her tour of a centuries old pirates' lair in St. Malo. They planned to be back at the end of the week, after which, they would live and work on Gérard's parents' farm near Sainte Suzanne for a year until the Desbois' were ready to retire to Sillé le Guillaume. Then, the young couple would take over the farm and manage it by themselves.

The following Sunday, the whole family went in to Evron as usual and I accompanied Madame Bardou and her youngest daughter to church. The priest devoted his sermon to what he called, "one of the great messages of the Gospel," stressing the importance of Jesus' Sermon on the Mount, in which he said, *"Blessed are those who are persecuted for righteousness' sake, for theirs is the kingdom of Heaven."*

After the Mass, I asked Madame Bardou if I could speak to the priest for a few minutes and meet her at the café afterward. She said I could and I went to the rectory to find the priest. I asked him if he could spare a moment to answer a couple of questions and he invited me to take a seat.

"Father," I said, "in your sermon today, you referred to the passage in the Sermon on the Mount which says, *"Blessed are those who are persecuted,"* and I would like to ask you whether this applies also to those who are persecuted by the Germans today, the members of the *Résistance*, the Gypsies and the Jews."

"Certainly, my son; it applies to all who are mistreated and made to suffer for no fault of their own . . . And that includes the Gypsies and the Jews.

"Since you ask this, Michel, I imagine you have a special reason for doing so. Do you know any Jews being persecuted at this time?"

"Yes, Father," I said, "I had a few Jewish friends

who lived on my street in Bagnolet, and one morning, last year, the police arrested them and their entire families. Later we learned that they were sent to a labor camp. Would that be regarded as an act of persecution?"

"Yes, my son," said the priest, "that is *persecution*, and that is why the Lord said that in the sight of God, they are 'blessed,' because they are the unfortunate victims of unwarranted hatred."

"Father, there is another question I would like to ask you. Is it true that Jews and Gypsies belong to an inferior race, and that the Germans are the members of a superior race, as they claim?"

"No, my son; it's not true. No group of people can claim superiority over another. We are all equal in God's sight and will be judged by Him one day according to our merit and the good deeds we have performed, and *not* in accordance with the erroneous beliefs of some dictator."

"May I ask you a last question, Father? Why do the authorities say that the Jews and the Gypsies should be punished for their wickedness?"

He looked at me kindly for a moment and said: "The Nazis, and those who emulate them, are mistaken and misguided. What some members of the Jewish people may have done a long time ago should not be a reason for persecuting them today. The Lord has asked us to forgive everyone, Michel."

"Thank you, Father. These things had been troubling me for some time. Now I must rejoin the Bardous who are taking care of me while my mother is in Paris."

"I appreciate your coming to talk to me about my sermon, Michel" said the priest. "Please, don't hesitate to ask whenever you have a question."

Today, I am sure the priest must have known or suspected that I was a Jewish by the kinds of questions I asked, but to his credit, he never made any attempt to probe my real identity, for had he done so, I might have confessed the truth to him. I knew that I was not to disclose my identity to anyone because it might jeopardize my cover and endanger the lives of those who were taking care of me. But I was glad I could speak about these matters with the priest just the same; for I sensed that he was a kind person with a genuine concern for the well-being of everyone who came to him.

XIII
The Last Year of the Occupation

DURING MY MOTHER'S LAST VISIT, I learned much about what was happening in Paris and with the war. The German army was losing ground on all fronts and the Allies were liberating one region after another. The end of the war was in sight, but the persecution of the Jews was worse than ever. Jewish families were now being arrested and deported in even greater numbers.

Early in 1944, Joseph Damant, the head of a paramilitary organization called the Milice was made Secretary General for the Maintenance of Order in France. Soon after, the Vichy government put the Milice in charge of arresting Jews, replacing the French and German police in most cases. The militiamen were ruthless in the performance of their new assignment and didn't even bother to coordinate their plans with the French police, accusing them of being lax in the execution of their duties.

As the Soviet armies advanced on the Eastern Front, approaching the borders of Romania, the Romanian government, which had been collaborating with the Germans until now, suddenly changed its allegiance and joined the Soviet camp. As a consequence, the Germans ordered the Milice to arrest all Jews who currently held Romanian passports, and all Romanians were now treated as enemies of the Third Reich.

The Marcus family that lived only a few blocks from us was immediately arrested and deported. The

Rubinsteins, however, had come up with an elaborate plan of escape in case of such an emergency. Upon hearing some unusual noise in the street one morning, they immediately left their house through the back door and went into their yard. Using an old garden chair as a platform, they jumped over the fence into their neighbor's yard and quickly rushed to the little gate at the other end of the property. They found the key hidden under a mat and opened the gate which led into an alley. They crossed the alley and entered the yard of a carpenter who kept piles of construction materials scattered all around his workshop. Sneaking between two big piles of lumber, they immediately lay down and covered themselves with a brown tarpaulin and stayed there until it was safe to come out.

The Milice searched their house and interrogated the neighbors before finally giving up. An hour later, the carpenter let the Rubensteins know that they could come out; the Milice had left the neighborhood. They waited quietly in the workshop until nightfall, and then proceeded according to the plan they had arranged several months before. The carpenter put them in the back of his truck, placed some lumber in front of them, and he took them to a convent in the east side of Paris.

The Mother Superior of the convent had agreed to let them spend a night or two at the convent in case of an emergency. They knocked at the side door of the convent with the proper signal and a nun came running to open the door. Quickly, they entered the convent and were led to a guest room where they spent the night.

The next morning, the nuns arranged for them to be taken to a small village in Burgundy. The uncle of one of the nuns owned a cottage on the outskirts of the village that had been empty for several years, and the Rubinsteins were able to stay there for a while. They would never have been able to escape without the cooperation of their neighbors, the intervention of the Mother Superior of the convent, and the uncle of one of the nuns. All of them had been willing to risk their lives to save a Jewish family.

When the Milice came for the Levis, they were caught by surprise and had no way of escaping. The militiamen knocked at their door and shouted, "Open, police!" and Mr. Levi knew he had only eight or ten seconds before they would force the door. He took his two children, seven and nine years old, and told them to hide under his bed and to be quite; then he went to open the door. After verifying their identity, the militiamen gave them two minutes to gather some clothes. Mr. and Mrs. Levi were then taken away, leaving their children behind. The children waited all day for their parents to return and then went to sleep in their own bed.

The next morning, realizing that their parents had not come back, they got dressed and left the apartment. They crossed the corridor and knocked on the door of their neighbor's apartment to ask if they knew where their parents might be. When Henry Perrier opened the door and saw the children standing in front of him, he could barely believe what he was seeing. He thought they had been arrested with their parents the day before. He invited them into his apartment and promptly closed the door so that no one would know that the children were still in the building. The Perriers, both retired civil servants, realized the gravity of the situation immediately.

"You are welcome in our home," said Monsieur Perrier to the children, "but no one must know that you are here. I'm going to look for a family or a children's home where you may be looked after until your parents' return. From now on, no one must know that you are

Jewish, because that would place both you and your benefactors in great danger. You must know that the *Boches* (Germans) and their friends have no pity for Jewish children. I suggest you refrain from using the name Levi, because it would tell people that you are Jewish. From now on, call yourselves Lévéque instead; this is a typical Christian name. I know that all of these things are difficult tasks, but you know that we are in the middle of a war and we have to do strange things sometimes in order to avoid being caught by the police."

"You really think, Monsieur Perrier, that our parents will not come back today or tomorrow?" asked the elder of the two children.

"I don't think they will; most of the people who are arrested are later deported to Germany."

Madame Perrier then said to the children: "You will have to go back to the apartment and collect some clothes in a little suitcase just as if you were going to summer camp."

"I will take one or two of my books also," said Jonathan, "and Sonia will probably want to take her teddy bear."

"You can't go just yet," said Madame Perrier, "as someone may see you and report you to the police. We will have to wait until evening, when most people are at home eating dinner and no one is in the stairway. You will have to enter the apartment in the dark and draw the curtains; only then can you put on a small light in order to gather your clothes. I will come and help you."

That evening, Madame Perrier and the children went to the apartment and returned with the two suitcases. The children thanked Monsieur and Madame Perrier for their kindness and prepared to spend the night on a couch. They certainly missed their parents, but soon fell asleep in their new environment. The

Perriers did their best to provide some comfort to the children for a few weeks until they were eventually placed in a Catholic orphanage.

When I asked my mother why the Perriers had risked so much for the children, she said: "Leo . . . I should say 'Michel' . . . You should know by now that most French people have good hearts and are ready to do whatever is needed to save innocent people, especially children, whenever they can."

"But Jews," I said, "are being denounced by their French neighbors and arrested by the police all the time."

"Yes, that's true; but only by a small number of people filled with hatred, or out of greed." Then she added: "The next time I come, I hope I will have better news to share with you. The war is slowly coming to an end. The Allies are progressing on all fronts and the Nazis are retreating despite their claims of having an 'invincible' army. May God continue to protect us!"

My mother returned to Paris while I stayed on at the farm wondering what the next day would bring. In the mean time, I would go into the fields with the farmer and his sons and try to help in some way. We would work until early afternoon and then return to the farm. If the animals had already been fed, I would take a walk around the farm and think about my mother and my grandmother and all our friends, and I would ask God to watch over them.

The following Sunday, after the Mass, there was a great deal of excitement in the cafe. One of the farmers from Mezangers had brought in an old map (dated from the first World War) and was pointing-out all the cities on the Russian and Italian fronts that had been liberated by the Allies. I had never seen the farmers so engrossed. They were assessing the difficulties the allied armies would face in order to liberate some of the territories which were still occupied by the Germans. They were not well informed about the strength of the German army, but they knew that much depended upon the quality of the terrain the Allies would have to cross in order to pursue their enemy. Some of the farmers had been following the progress of the allied forces since the beginning of the war and were explaining to us what some of the obstacles might be.

Those who listened to the BBC broadcasts on a regular basis also reported that the American and British High Commands had hinted that they were about to create a new front on the west coast of France! But the Germans were aware of it and had begun to amass troops all along the seashores of Normandy. References were made to a place called "Omaha Beach," but no one knew where that might be.

The owner of the café added to the excitement by offering a free round of drinks to all his customers when the Allies liberated a major city. Thus we had begun to celebrate the beginning of the end after four long years.

XIV
The Liberation

IN THE EARLY SPRING OF 1944, the Allies succeeded in establishing a beachhead on the coast of Normandy on D-Day. The Atlantic Wall, which the Germans had built-up along the northern Atlantic coast for several years, simply could not resist the power of the American bombs which were dropped on it. Though the Allies suffered many casualties, their troops were now advancing steadily on French territory, liberating one city after another.

The American advance caused great excitement in France. After four years of German occupation, the prospect of living in freedom once again made us tremble with anticipation. At the farm, we began planning a little ceremony to celebrate the coming victory of the Allies. In the event the Americans or the British troops were to come our way, we prepared several bottles of the finest cider and apple brandy for them.

At the same time, the German and French police began to relax their control over the civilian population. There were fewer deportations now, simply because the Germans could not find enough trains for them. All available resources were now needed to transport troops and supplies to strengthen their military posts at the Western front.

As the allied troops advanced toward Laval, my mother came to Sainte Gemmes le Robert to bring my brother and me back to Paris, fearing that the whole area might become a battlefield. I gathered my belongings excitedly and came back to the house as quickly as my legs would carry me. We kissed each other goodbye and I thanked the Bardous for their warm hospitality to me. But just as we were about to leave the farm for good, Madame Bardou stopped my mother and asked her discretely: "Madame Leon, I'd like to ask you a question. Would you tell us the real reason you asked us to take your son? Is it because you are Jewish and were afraid that you might be arrested and deported to the camps?"

At that moment, my mother burst into tears and said, somewhat haltingly: *"Yes, Madame Bardou!* I did not want my children to be arrested and sent to the death camps! My mother and I took a great risk remaining in Paris, but I wanted the boys to have a chance to grow up and live their lives—even if *we* were arrested. We will be forever indebted to you for your generosity. May God bless you!"

"Madame Leon," she said, "we only did what was right, and we are glad that your son was safe with us. It was a pleasure having him around the farm, helping out whenever possible. I think he could become a good farmer one day if he wants to do that. You will always be welcome at the farm whenever you come to visit. *Au Revoir!"*

Monsieur Bardou took us to Evron and dropped us in front of Madame Lemaître's shoe store.

We went into the store and my mother said: "Madame, I want to thank you for your kindness, and your willingness to assist us when we were in a difficult situation. I am especially grateful for the hospitality you showed me when I needed it most. May God bless you!"

"My friend, I am glad I was able to assist you on

occasion. I only did what my religion has enjoined me to do, to help my neighbor whenever possible. But let me tell you, Madame, that from the moment you first entered my store over a year ago, I knew that you must be Jewish and trying to avoid being arrested by the police. It is precisely for that reason that I decided to help you! Good luck, and may the future bring good tidings to you and all of us!"

As we came to the church, I asked my mother and my brother to come with me as I said goodbye to the priest. We went directly to the rectory and rang the bell. The priest opened the door and invited us to take a seat in the anteroom.

After we had seated ourselves, I said, "Father, I wanted you to meet my mother and my brother before we return to Paris."

"Madame Leon," he said, "I am delighted to meet you, and to tell you that your son is a good boy, and that he acted with reverence toward me and the church with which I am associated. It was not difficult to guess that Michel was Jewish — even though he made a good effort to pretend that he was simply the child of a non-practicing Catholic family!"

Then he said: "I really want to commend you; it was good thinking on your part to place him with one of our local farm families, most of whom do not approve of the Vichy government and its persecution of the Jews. May God bless you!"

"Father," I said, "I am very grateful to you for your willingness to answer my questions. Your kindness was very comforting to me."

"Remember, my son, we are *all* God's children; whether we be Catholic or Jewish, God cares for all of us."

We returned to Paris on the next train. To our great surprise, we found that there was not a single policeman on duty at the station!

After Normandy and Brittany were liberated, the Allies set out for Paris. But many changes were already taking place in the capital. The Commissary on Jewish Affairs, and the official spokesman for the police, made announcements on the radio and in the press that Jews could now remove the yellow stars from their clothing and no longer needed special permission to travel.

It was not difficult for us to understand the reason for the sudden change in attitude: the government did not want the Allies to see how badly they had mistreated the Jews during the occupation. In fact, everyone who had collaborated with the Germans was suddenly anxious about the future. Many were afraid they would be arrested and brought to justice by the new government that would be established after the Occupation. Many planned to plead innocence, claiming that they were simply obeying the orders of their superiors. And their superiors, in turn, were planning to place the blame for all the arrests they were forced to carry out on the Nazis.

It was now only a matter of days before Paris would be liberated. As one city after another was wrested from the Germans by the Allies, we could hardly tear ourselves from our radio receivers. The excitement was palpable everywhere, and once again, I could share in the life of the city as an equal citizen.

I soon went back to my college and tried to catch up with the studies I had missed in the last year and a half. In my class, a large map was spread across the blackboard, and we followed the advance of the allied armies by placing little flags on all the cities which had been liberated. There was still fighting in a number of regions, but it seemed that the German troops could do nothing but retreat. The morale of their soldiers was low and a growing number were surrendering to the Allies everyday.

As the liberation of France seemed imminent, the frustrated feelings of anger at the Germans which had been simmering for years, now began to erupt in displays of open defiance. In the last few days of the occupation, a number of people even took it upon themselves to attack German soldiers at random in the streets of Paris. As a result, many were killed by these German soldiers who were simply more experienced and better equipped. These indiscriminate attacks did not serve any particular military objective and cost the lives of a few hundred French citizens.

Around this time, I witnessed a gun battle in the street as I was coming back from school. I saw several people shot and killed only a few yards from where I was standing. I took shelter in a dark entrance to a building from which I could still see what was happening in the street. The bodies of the dead and the wounded lay bloody on the pavement.

After the Germans left, a few courageous men went out to the aid of the wounded and remove the dead from the street while we waited for the ambulances to arrive. I came out of my hiding place and regretted that I was too young and inexperienced to know how to help the wounded. Soon, the ambulances arrived and the crowd dispersed as the dead and wounded were taken away.

As one walks through the streets of Paris today, one can see plaques affixed to various buildings which tell of French patriots who were killed at that very place during the last days of the Occupation. And from time

143

to time, someone places a flower on the plaque to honor their memory and sacrifice.

In a symbolic gesture, my mother retrieved the gun that had belonged to my grandfather and which he had kept as a souvenir from World War I. We had buried it in the courtyard in front of our house soon after the Germans invaded because it was strictly forbidden to own a gun. When we unearthed it, however, we saw that it was completely rusted and could no longer serve any purpose.

By the end of July, as the Allies rapidly approached the capital, we heard that the Germans were threatening to destroy all the historic monuments of Paris before leaving the city. Fortunately, an agreement was reached between the Germans and the Allies which stipulated that the Germans would be allowed to leave Paris unharmed, and 90 minutes later, the American, British and French troops would enter the capital.

On that day, hundreds of people gathered on the Boulevard Mortier. We watched triumphantly as the last German soldiers crowded on trucks and armored vehicles and left the city in haste. We then waited in silence for an hour and a half until the first American tank appeared. At the site of it, we cheered ecstatically.

This first tank was followed by more, until a whole column of armored vehicles was moving along the boulevard. When they neared the square where we had gathered to salute them, they stopped their engines and emerged from the tanks to greet the jubilant crowd. Their faces were beaming with pride and joy; after all, it was their moment as much as it was ours.

Some of them had learned a few words of French, but most were simply communicating with gestures and distributing gifts. I was standing next to a tank as its commander came out of the hatch and smiled at us. He shook hands with us and said a few words we didn't understand as he gave us some candy and chewing gum. As I looked at him, I noticed that he had a silver Star of David attached to his dog tags. I stared in amazement for a moment before he noticed me and asked in Yiddish, *"Du bist a Yid?"* — Are you Jewish?

"Yah," I said, *"Ich bin a Yid!"* — Yes, *I am* a Jew!

His mouth opened wide with joy and he quickly lifted me into the air and put me on the tank! We chatted in Yiddish for a long time, two Jews from different parts of the world, talking openly in the streets of Paris, both having fulfilled 'the Eleventh Commandment' — *to survive.*

Leo Abramowski in 1944 after the liberation of Paris.

Afterword

AFTER THE LIBERATION OF PARIS, I was fortunate enough to be able to resume my studies at College Turgot.

When I was fifteen, I finally celebrated my *bar mitzvah*—which had been impossible during the war—and enrolled in a teachers' program at the Séminaire Israélite de France in Paris. I graduated five years later as a cantor and teacher of religion.

I then took a position at the Grande Synagogue in Geneva, Switzerland, where I officiated as cantor and taught in their religious school. I did this for seven years, while also studying psychology and education at the Charles Baudouin Institute of Psychoanalysis and the Institut Jean-Jacques Rousseau.

In my last year, I married an American exchange student from San Francisco and decided to move to the United States, where I studied at Hebrew Union College in Cincinnati, the oldest and largest rabbinical seminary in the country.

After earning a Master's degree in Hebrew Letters and being ordained as a rabbi in 1963, I accepted a post in Guatemala-City and later in Curaçao before returning to the United States. I then served as a rabbi in Berkeley and Long Beach, California, and during an interim of three years, in Sandton, South Africa, during the dismantling of apartheid. After moving to Arizona and serving for five more years as a pulpit rabbi, I finally retired.

Today, I live with my wife Rosemary in Sun City West on the outskirts of Phoenix where I continue to write and teach about Judaism and Jewish history.

About the Author

LEO MICHEL ABRAMI is a semi-retired rabbi living in Phoenix, Arizona. He teaches at the Jewish Studies Institute, the Arizona Institute of Logotherapy, and the ASU Lifelong Learning Institute of Sun City.

He has previously published a French introduction to Logotherapy (the psychotherapeutic method initiated by Viktor Frankl), contributed to a book on the Dead Sea Scrolls and an essay on the psychology of Jewish humor to *Best Jewish Writings 2003*. He has also published a number of articles in the *International Forum for Logotherapy, Midstream Magazine, the Jewish Bible Quarterly, the Journal of Spirituality in Mental Health,* and *The Journal of Ecumenical Studies.* He is currently preparing a collection of Jewish stories, a mnemonic method for learning to read Hebrew, and researching a book on the Jewish presence in the New Testament.

He can be reached at leoabrami@hotmail.com.

www.ingramcontent.com/pod-product-compliance
Lightning Source LLC
LaVergne TN
LVHW092323080426
835508LV00039B/515